A *Garden* OF *Shawls*

Karen Whooley

OCCHI BLU
PRESS

isbn: 978-0-9723232-2-2
eBook isbn: 978-0-9723232-3-9

Technical editor: Kj Hay
Model crocheters: Amy Curtin,
Penny Shima Glanz, Karen Whooley
Photography: Anne Podlesak
Model: Theresa Martinez
Book design: Elizabeth Green

To David, Tyler and Cassandra.

"Be who God meant you to be and
you will set the world on fire."

—St. Catherine of Siena

Contents

Introduction

Welcome to *A Garden of Shawls*. In these pages you will find 12 gorgeous shawls inspired by my love of Italian lace and interesting construction. If you are looking for an elegant accessory for a night on the town, something comfortable with jeans, warmth on a cool night or just something fun to wear, I am sure you will find what you are looking for between the covers of this book!

From the time I was seven years old I have been fascinated with crochet lace. That summer I learned to crochet, my Nonna gave me a size 6 steel hook – 1.8 mm for those who are wondering – and some size 10 crochet cotton thread and I learned traditional Italian laces.

As I got older I fell away from working in the tiny threads for many years but I still had a fascination with lace and open work of all sorts. And as I moved through my design career, using simple constructions with lace have been a favorite tool I have used in many of my original designs. I have included some of my favorite ways to create a shawl.

This book is for every crocheter who is comfortable with the basic crochet stitches. Every pattern includes charts, a special stitches section as well as text so you can easily work your way through the pattern. There are also sections at the beginning of the book for abbreviations, hints and information on how to make these shawls work with heavier yarns.

I know you will enjoy every minute of your journey in my *Garden of Shawls*! Let's get started!

Before You Get Started

Gauge

Gauge is probably the dirty word of crochet. Most of us don't like to take the time or, as I have heard in some of my classes, waste the yarn to check our gauge. But – especially in my experience with lace crochet – gauge can be the difference between a shawl that is just right and one that will cover an African elephant.

When looking at the gauge and which hook I recommend for each pattern remember that the hook size is just that: a recommendation. I may be a looser crocheter than you. You may have to go to a hook that is 2–3 times larger to get the same gauge. That is OK! If you have to go down a hook size to get the gauge, that is fine!

And don't forget ... every pattern's gauge is the BLOCKED gauge. So not only will you need to make a swatch, you will need to block it.

Substituting Heavier Yarns

I realize that there are many of you who don't like the finer yarns I used in this book. That is absolutely fine! You can substitute a heavier weight yarn but that means gauge is going to be even more important!

A heavier yarn means that your shawl will grow longer and wider faster than the pattern is written. But every pattern has a repeat. So what you would need to do is make a gauge swatch following the pattern for at least 3 repeats. Block it. Then measure your gauge. You will have to do some math using your gauge to figure out how many repeats you will need in order for your shawl to come out the size and depth you want it to be.

There are a couple of things to note about using heavier yarns than what I used. First, the shawl will be bulkier than what the models look like. You will need to play with hook sizes to be able to get some good drape on the heavier shawls. And secondly, the yarn requirements will be vastly different that what I included in the pattern. Most will have less yardage but only a good gauge swatch will help you figure it out.

Reading a Crochet Chart

I believe that everyone learns to read patterns differently. Some people are very visual; others can get by with just the words. That is why you will find every pattern in this book includes both written instructions and symbol charts.

To read my charts, the first thing you want to look at is the key. Each symbol represents a stitch in the pattern. It's important that you know how to make all of the stitches shown in the key. If you don't, check the special stitches section of the pattern to learn how.

You will always read the crochet chart from bottom to top. Every row or round is numbered where it begins. The odd rows will be one color, the even another. Both of these will help you to keep from losing your place. If you are working in rows, you will turn the work at the end of every row. If you are working in rounds, most often you will continue to work on the right side of the fabric. But verify in the written pattern

that this is the case as often there are patterns that do need to turn the work in the round.

Normally you will only be working into a chain when you are working into the foundation chain. However, if you see one or more stitches sitting on top of one or multiple chains that will indicate that you will work in the chain space not in the chain(s) themselves. But use your written pattern to be sure that is the case.

If you are working solely from the chart, you might want to use a ruler, a magnetic chart keeper or even removable highlighter tape to keep track of the row you are on. If you are in the middle of the row, using a removeable flag to point out the stitch you are at can also be very helpful.

When in doubt, you can always refer back to the text of the pattern. I find that this is the best way to figure out tricky parts of the pattern.

Abbreviations

blo	back loops only	sc	single crochet
ch	chain	sk	skip
dc	double crochet	sp(s)	space(s)
dtr	double treble crochet	sl st	slip stitch
hdc	half double crochet	st(s)	stitch(es)
rnd(s)	round(s)	tr	triple crochet

Blocking

Blocking is your friend! Truly! The reason you want to block your shawl is twofold:

- ❧ All of my gauges and finished sizes are to blocked measurements.

- ❧ Blocking your fabric will open up your the spaces in the lace and create beautiful draping fabric.

Every one of the shawls has been firmly blocked and you will want to do the same with your shawls! Never blocked before? Here is how:

Start by soaking your shawl in cool water with a little bit of gentle detergent for at least 30 minutes. Once the fabric is thoroughly wet, place the shawl inside a large towel, roll it up and squeeze gently to remove the excess water. You want the fabric wet but not dripping.

Once the excess water is gone, lay out your shawl on your blocking surface. I use blocking mats but you can use a bed, carpet, or any other such soft surface. If you have blocking wires, weave them through the top edge of the shawl that lays against your neck. If you don't, you can skip this step.

Using the schematic for the shawl as your guide, pin out the straight, top edge. Make sure to tug the fabric well to start opening up the lacework. I use a yardstick or tape measure (sometimes both for extra long items) to make sure everything is straight and even. Use non-rusting T-Pins for the best results.

Once the top is straight, loosely pin out either side of the shawl to make sure that part stays in place and remains straight if it is a wider edge. If you have wires, here is another place to put them. Next pin out the bottom edge to size. This is where you will have to really tug well to open up everything. If you have an edging that is rippled or has points or even picots, you will want to place a pin in each peak to make sure they stand open the way they need to be.

Now comes the hard part. LET. IT. DRY. Let it dry completely! In some areas you may have more humidity in your air and it will take longer than others. But if you wait, you will be very happy with the results. Once the fabric is completely dry, carefully unpin.

Incipient

By definition, Incipient is something about to happen. As with a spring garden, our Incipient shawl is reminiscent of a gardening starting to bud. A simple shawl in lace weight yarn and worked from side to side with a bud-laden edging at the same time, your love affair with shawls will begin.

Skill Level

Intermediate

Finished Size

Blocked – 63 inches (160 cm) wide by 14 inches (36 cm) deep at longest point

Materials

1200 yards (1098 m) 2-ply laceweight yarn

Model uses The Fiber Seed Silky Seed Lace (50% fine merino / 50% tussah silk; 600 yds / 1594 m = 6 oz / 120g) in colorways #SSL009 Shamrock (Color A) and #SSL003 Dragon Fruit (Color B)

US size E/5 (3.5mm) crochet hook or size needed for gauge

Yarn needle

Gauge

24 dc and 12 dc rows = 4 inches (10 cm) when blocked

Special Stitches

Dc2tog: Double crochet 2 together: [Yarn over, insert hook in next stitch and pull up a loop, yarn over and draw through 2 loops on hook] twice, yarn over and draw through all 3 loops on hook.

Fdc: Foundation double crochet (This technique creates a foundation chain and a row of double crochet stitches in one) –

Step 1: Place a slip knot on hook, ch 2, yarn over, insert hook in 2nd ch from hook and draw up a loop; yarn over and draw through one loop on hook (the "chain"); [yarn over and draw through 2 loops on hook] 2 times (the "double crochet").

Step 2: Yarn over, insert hook into the "chain" of the previous stitch and draw up a loop, yarn over and draw through one loop on hook (the "chain"), [yarn over and draw through 2 loops on hook] 2 times (the "double crochet"). Repeat step 2 for the length of foundation.

picot: Ch 3, sl st in first ch made.

First Edge Leaf: (Tr, [ch 1, tr] twice, ch 3, tr, [ch 1, tr] twice) in sp between Rows 2 and 3, sl st in base of first fdc of Row 1, turn. 3 sc in each of next 2 ch-1 sps, (4 sc, picot, 4 sc) in next ch-3 sp, 3 sc in each of next 2 ch-1 sps, sl st in top of last dc worked before the Edge Leaf.

Edge Leaf: (Tr, [ch 1, tr] twice, ch 3, tr, [ch 1, tr] twice) in sp between rows 2 rows below, sl st in same st as last sl st of previous Edge Leaf, turn. 3 sc in each of next 2 ch-1 sps, (4 sc, picot, 4 sc) in next ch-3 sp, 3 sc in each of next 2 ch-1 sps, sl st in top of last dc worked before the Edge Leaf.

Note: A space between rows 2 rows below is the space between the row numbered 2 less than the row you are currently working and the row numbered 1 less than the row you are currently working. For example, if you are working Row 8, the space between rows 2 rows below is between Row 8-2 = Row 6 and Row 8-1 = Row 7.

Pattern Notes

The ch-2 turning chain does not count as a stitch. You will work your first dc in the first dc of every row.

The first 2 dc in every odd row and the last 2 dc in every even row as well as the Edge Leaf is done in Color A. The remaining dc in the main field of the shawl is done in color B.

Directions

Increase Section

Row 1: With Color A, make 2 fdc changing to color B to complete the last stitch; make 10 more fdc; ch 2, turn. (12 fdc)

Row 2: With Color B, dc in next 9 dc, 2 dc in next dc changing to color A to complete the last stitch, dc in last 2 dc, ch 2, turn. (13 dc)

Row 3: With Color A, dc in first 2 dc changing to color B to complete the last st, dc in each dc across, ch 2, turn.

Note: Continue to work first 2 sts of odd-numbered rows and last 2 sts of even-numbered rows with A and remaining sts with color B throughout.

Row 4: Dc in next 10 dc, 2 dc in next dc, dc in last 2 dc, do not turn, work First Edge Leaf; ch 2, turn. (14 dc and 1 Edge Leaf)

Row 5: Dc in each dc across, ch 2, turn.

Row 6: Dc in each dc to last 3 dc, 2 dc in next dc, dc in each of last 2 dc; ch 2, turn. (15 dc)

Row 7: Dc in each dc across, ch 2, turn.

Row 8: Dc in each dc to last 3 dc, 2 dc in next dc, dc in each of last 2 dc do not turn, work Edge Leaf; ch 2, turn. (16 dc and 1 Edge Leaf)

Rows 9–84: Repeat rows 5–8 19 times more. (54 dc and 1 Edge Leaf at the end of row 84)

Center Section

Row 85–87: Dc in each dc across, ch 2, turn.

Row 88: Dc in each dc across, do not turn, work Edge Leaf; ch 2, turn.

Rows 89–96: Rep rows 85–88 twice more.

Decrease Section

Row 97: Dc in each dc across, ch 2, turn.

Row 98: Dc in each dc to last 4 dc, dc2tog, dc in each of last 2 dc; ch 2, turn. (53 dc)

Row 99: Dc in each dc across, ch 2, turn.

Row 100: Dc in each dc to last 4 dc, dc2tog, dc in each of last 2 dc do not turn, work Edge Leaf; ch 2, turn. (52 dc and 1 Edge Leaf)

Rows 101–180: Repeat rows 97-100 twenty times more. Fasten off. (12 dc at the end of row 180)

Finishing

Weave in all ends. Lightly block to dimensions.

63 inches

SHAWL

14 inches

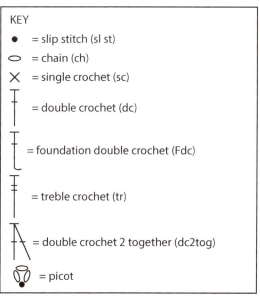

KEY

- ● = slip stitch (sl st)
- ⬭ = chain (ch)
- ✕ = single crochet (sc)
- ╤ = double crochet (dc)
- ╤ = foundation double crochet (Fdc)
- ╪ = treble crochet (tr)
- ⅄ = double crochet 2 together (dc2tog)
- ⬭ = picot

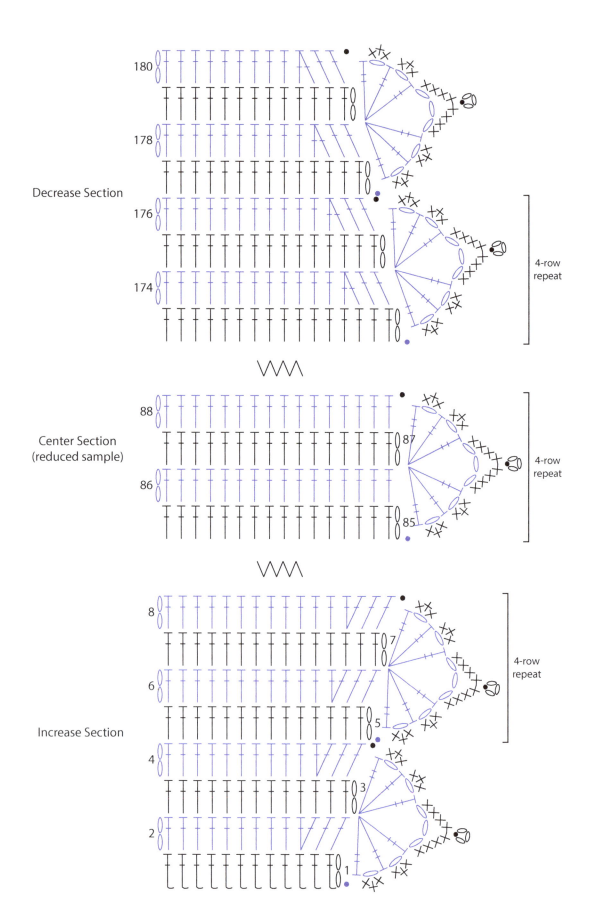

Decrease Section

180
178
176
174

4-row
repeat

Center Section
(reduced sample)

88
87
86
85

4-row
repeat

Increase Section

8
7
6
5
4
3
2
1

4-row
repeat

Palisade

A Palisade is a type of wall or fence that defines a space, such as a white picket fence in a garden. Our palisade shawl is a simple but elegant crescent worked from side to side including the edging. This beauty can add soft curves to jeans and a t-shirt or a colorful day dress.

Skill Level

Intermediate

Finished Size

Approximately 67 inches (170 cm) wide by 17 inches (43 cm) deep at longest point when blocked

Materials

860 yards (786 m) 2-ply laceweight yarn

Model uses Black Trillium Fibres Silken Lace (85% superwash merino / 15% mulberry silk; 7.05 oz / 200g = 1450 yds / 1326 m) in the colorway Lemon Chiffon

Size 3.0 mm crochet hook or size needed for gauge

Stitch marker
Yarn needle

Gauge

19 dc and 13 dc rows = 4 inches (10 cm) when blocked

Special Stitches

3-dc Cl: Three double crochet cluster – Yarn over, insert hook in indicated stitch or space and draw up a loop, yarn over and draw through 2 loops on hook (2 loops remain on hook); [yarn over, insert hook in same stitch or space and draw up a loop, yarn over and draw through 2 loops on hook] 2 times; yarn over and draw through all 4 loops on hook.

X-st: Sk next ch-1 sp, dc in next ch-1 sp, ch 1, working over the top of dc just worked, dc in skipped ch-1 sp.

Dc2tog: Double crochet 2 together: [Yarn over, insert hook in next stitch and pull up a loop, yarn over and draw through 2 loops on hook] twice, yarn over and draw through all 3 loops on hook.

Pattern Notes

Ch2 at the beg of each even row does not count as a stitch. Always work first double crochet in the first stitch.

Directions

Ch 45, place Stitch Marker in 3rd ch from hook for stitch placement.

Increase Section

Row 1: Dc in 8th ch from hook, [ch 2, sk next 2 ch, dc in next ch] 3 times for lace edging, ch 1, sk next ch, dc in next ch, [sk 2 ch, dc in next ch, ch 1, working across the front of dc just made, dc in first skipped ch, dc in next ch] 5 times for textured band, ch 1, sk next ch, dc in last 5 ch for dc-body of shawl. (5 dc and 4 ch-2 sps in lace edging; 5 X-sts in textured band; 5 dc in body)

Row 2: Ch 2, turn, dc in next 3 dc, 2 dc in next dc, dc in next dc, ch 1, sk next ch-1 sp, dc in next dc, [ch 1, 3-dc-cl in next ch-1 sp, ch 1, sk next dc, dc in next dc] 5 times, ch 1, sk next ch-1 sp, dc in next dc, [2 dc in next ch-2 sp, dc in next dc] 3 times, 2 dc in next ch-7 sp, dc in marked ch (leave marker). (13 dc in lace edging; 5 clusters in textured band; 6 dc in body)

Row 3: Ch 9, turn, dc in first dc, [ch 2, sk next 2 dc, dc in next dc] 4 times, ch 1, sk ch-1 sp. dc in next dc, [X-st, dc in next dc] 5 times, ch 1, sk ch-1 sp, dc in each dc to end. (5 dc, 4 ch-2 sps, and 1 ch-9 sp in lace edging; 5 X-sts in textured band; 6 dc in body)

Row 4: Ch 2, turn, dc in each dc to last 2 dc before first ch-1 sp, 2 dc in next dc, dc in next dc, ch 1, sk next ch-1 sp, [dc in next dc, ch 1, 3-dc-cl in next

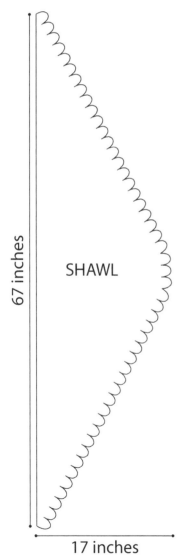

67 inches

SHAWL

17 inches

ch-1 sp, ch 1, sk next dc, dc in next dc] 5 times, ch 1, sk next ch-1 sp, dc in next dc, [2 dc in next ch-2 sp, dc in next dc] 4 times, 13 dc in next ch-9 sp, sl st in marked ch (remove marker). (26 dc in lace edging; 5 clusters in textured band; 7 dc in body)

Row 5: Ch 3, turn, sk first dc, [sc in next dc, ch 3, sk next dc] 6 times, sl st in next dc, ch 5, place marker in 3rd ch from hook for stitch placement, sk next 2 dc, dc in next dc, [ch 2, sk next 2 dc, dc in next dc] 3 times, ch 1, sk ch-1 sp, dc in next dc, [X-st, dc in next dc] 5 times, ch 1, sk ch-1 sp, dc in each dc to end. (5 dc, 6 sc, 7 ch-3 sps, and 4 ch-2 sps in lace edging; 5 X-sts in textured band; 7 dc in body)

Row 6: Ch 2, turn, dc in each dc to last 2 dc before first ch-1 sp, 2 dc in next dc, dc in next dc, ch 1, sk next ch-1 sp, [dc in next dc, ch 1, 3-dc-cl in next ch-1 sp, ch 1, sk next dc, dc in next dc] 5 times, ch 1, sk next ch-1 sp, [2 dc in next ch-2 sp, dc in next dc] 3 times, 2 dc in next ch-5 sp, dc in marked ch (leave marker). (13 dc in lace edging; 5 clusters in textured band; 8 dc in body)

Rows 7–9: Rep rows 3–5. (5 dc, 6 sc, 7 ch-3 sps, and 4 ch-2 sps in lace edging; 5 X-sts in textured band; 9 dc in body) in row 9.

Rows 10–93: Rep rows 6–9 twenty-one times. (51 dc in body)

Center Section

Row 94: Ch 2, turn, dc in each dc to first ch-1 sp, ch 1, sk next ch-1 sp, [dc in next dc, ch 1, 3-dc-cl in next ch-1 sp, ch 1, sk next dc, dc in next dc] 5 times, ch 1, sk next ch-1 sp, [2 dc in next ch-2 sp, dc in next dc] 3 times, 2 dc in next ch-5 sp, dc in marked ch (leave marker).

Row 95: Ch 9, turn, dc in first dc, [ch 2, sk next 2 dc, dc in next dc] 4 times, ch 1, sk ch-1 sp. dc in next dc, [X-st, dc in next dc] 5 times, ch 1, sk ch-1 sp, dc in each dc to end.

Row 96: Ch 2, turn, dc in each dc to first ch-1 sp, ch 1, sk next ch-1 sp, [dc in next dc, ch 1, 3-dc-cl in next ch-1 sp, ch 1, sk next dc, dc in next dc] 5 times, ch 1, sk next ch-1 sp, dc in next dc, [2 dc in next ch-2 sp, dc in next dc] 4 times, 13 dc in next ch-9 sp, sl st in marked ch (remove marker).

Row 97: Ch 3, turn, sk first dc, [sc in next dc, ch 3, sk next dc] 6 times, sl st in next dc, ch 5, place marker in 3rd ch from hook for stitch placement, sk next 2 dc, dc in next dc, [ch 2, sk next 2 dc, dc in next dc] 3 times, ch 1, sk ch-1 sp, dc in next dc, [X-st, dc in next dc] 5 times, ch 1, sk ch-1 sp, dc in each dc to end.

Rows 98–105: Rep rows 94–97 twice more.

Decrease Section

Row 106: Ch 2, turn, dc in each dc to 3 sts before first ch-1 sp, dc2tog, dc in next dc, ch 1, sk next ch-1 sp, [dc in next dc, ch 1, 3-dc-cl in next ch-1 sp, ch 1, sk next dc, dc in next dc] 5 times, ch 1, sk next ch-1 sp, [2 dc in next ch-2 sp, dc in next dc] 3 times, 2 dc in next ch-5 sp, dc in marked ch (leave marker). (50 dc in body)

Row 107: Ch 9, turn, dc in first dc, [ch 2, sk next 2 dc, dc in next dc] 4 times, ch 1, sk ch-1 sp. dc in next dc, [X-st, dc in next dc] 5 times, ch 1, sk ch-1 sp, dc in each dc to end.

Row 108: Ch 2, turn, dc in each dc to 3 sts before first ch-1 sp, dc2tog, dc in next dc, ch 1, sk next ch-1 sp, [dc in next dc, ch 1, 3-dc-cl in next ch-1 sp, ch 1, sk next dc, dc in next dc] 5 times, ch 1, sk next ch-1 sp, dc in next dc, [2 dc in next ch-2 sp, dc in next dc] 4 times, 13 dc in next ch-9 sp, sl st in marked ch (remove marker). (49 dc in body)

Row 109: Ch 3, turn, sk first dc, [sc in next dc, ch 3, sk next dc] 6 times, sl st in next dc, ch 5, place marker in 3rd ch from hook for stitch placement, sk next 2 dc, dc in next dc, [ch 2, sk next 2 dc, dc in next dc] 3 times, ch 1, sk ch-1 sp, dc in next dc, [X-st, dc in next dc] 5 times, ch 1, sk ch-1 sp, dc in each dc to end.

Rows 110–197: Rep rows 106–109 twenty-two times more. (5 dc in body)

Fasten off.

Finishing

Weave in all ends. Block to finished size.

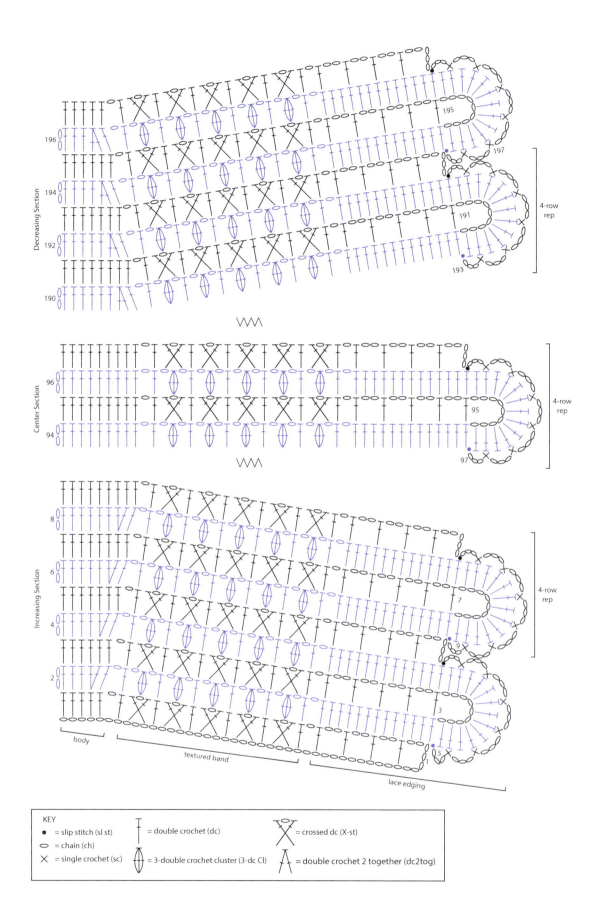

Decreasing Section

196

195

197

194

191

4-row rep

192

193

190

Center Section

96

95

94

4-row rep

97

Increasing Section

8

6

7

4-row rep

9

2

3

5

1

body

textured band

lace edging

KEY

● = slip stitch (sl st)

○ = chain (ch)

✕ = single crochet (sc)

† = double crochet (dc)

= 3-double crochet cluster (3-dc Cl)

= crossed dc (X-st)

= double crochet 2 together (dc2tog)

Trellis

Some flowers enjoy weaving in and out of a wooden structure or trellis as they reach for the sun. Garden Trellis like our Trellis shawl works best with a partner. Twining flowers like Morning Glories in the garden and summer wardrobes with the Trellis Shawl. This light and breezy crescent shaped shawlette can work together with your summer tops to add a bit of lacy elegance.

Skill Level

Easy

Finished Size

Approximately 65 inches (165 cm) wide by 15 inches (38 cm) deep at longest point when blocked.

Materials

550 yards (503 m) 2-ply laceweight yarn

Model uses Prism Yarns Lace Wool (100% wool; 3.5 oz / 100g = 1460 yds / 1335 m) in the colorway Arroyo

Size 3.0 mm crochet hook or size needed for gauge

Yarn needle

Gauge

24 dc and 12 dc rows = 4 inches (10 cm) when blocked

Special Stitches

dc2tog: Double crochet 2 together—[Yarn over, insert hook in next st and draw up a loop, yarn over and draw through 2 loops on hook] twice, yarn over and draw through all 3 loops on hook.

Pattern Notes

On all rows, if working into chain, work st(s) in back bump of ch.

Skipped chains at the beginning of odd-numbered rows count as ch-sps.

Directions

Ch 20.

Increase Section

Row 1: Dc in 8th ch from hook, dc in next 3 ch, [ch2, sk 2 ch, dc in next dc] twice, dc in last 3 ch. (9 dc and 3 ch-sps including the beginning ch-sp; the last 4 dc worked begin the body of the shawl, the other 5 dc and 3 ch-sps begin the lace edging)

Row 2: Ch 2, turn (does not count as st now and on all even rows), dc in first dc and in each dc to 2 dc before first ch-2 sp, 2 dc in next dc, dc in next dc, ch 2, [dc in next dc, ch 2] twice, sk 2 dc, dc in next dc, 3 dc in end ch-sp. (5 dc in body, 6 dc and 3 ch-sps in lace edging)

Row 3: Ch 9, turn, dc in 7th ch from hook, dc in next 2 ch, dc in next dc, ch 2, sk 2 dc, [dc in next dc, ch 2] 3 times, dc in each dc to end. (5 dc in body, 7 dc and 5 ch-sps in lace edging)

Row 4: Ch 2, turn, dc in first dc and in each dc to 2 dc before first ch-2 sp, 2 dc in next dc, dc in next dc, [ch 2, dc in next dc] 4 times, ch 2, sk 2 dc, dc in next dc, 3 dc in end ch-sp. (6 dc in body, 8 dc and 5 ch-sps in lace edging)

Row 5: Ch 9, turn, dc in 7th ch from hook, dc in next 2 ch, dc in next dc, ch 2, sk 2 dc, [dc in next dc, ch 2] 5 times, dc in each dc to end. (6 dc in body, 9 dc and 7 ch-sps in lace edging)

Row 6: Ch 2, turn, dc in first dc and in each dc to 2 dc before first ch-2 sp, 2 dc in next dc, dc in next dc, [ch 2, dc in next dc] 5 times, 2 dc in next ch-2 sp, dc in next dc; leave remaining sts unworked. (7 dc in body, 8 dc and 5 ch-sps in lace edging)

Row 7: Ch 5, sk first 3 dc, dc in next dc, 2 dc in next ch-2 sp, [dc in next dc, ch 2] 4 times,

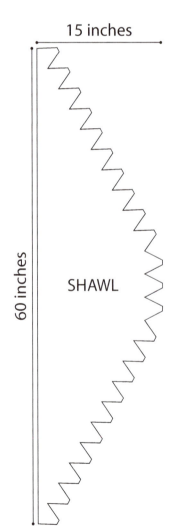

15 inches

60 inches

SHAWL

dc in each dc to end. (7 dc in body, 7 dc and 5 ch-sps in lace edging)

Row 8: Ch 2, turn, dc in first dc and in each dc to 2 dc before first ch-2 sp, 2 dc in next dc, dc in next dc, [ch 2, dc in next dc] 3 times, 2 dc in next ch-2 sp, dc in next dc; leave remaining sts unworked. (8 dc in body, 6 dc and 3 ch-sps in lace edging)

Row 9: Ch 5, sk first 3 dc, dc in next dc, 2 dc in next ch-2 sp, [dc in next dc, ch 2] twice, dc in each dc to end. (8 dc in body, 5 dc and 3 ch-sps in lace edging)

Rows 10–81: Rep rows 2–9 nine times. (44 dc in body, 5 dc and 3 ch-sps in lace edging) in row 81.

Center Section

Row 82: Ch 2, turn, dc in first dc and in each dc to first ch-2 sp, ch 2, [dc in next dc, ch 2] twice, sk 2 dc, dc in next dc, 3 dc in end ch-sp. (44 dc in body, 6 dc and 3 ch-sps in lace edging)

Row 83: Ch 9, turn, dc in 7th ch from hook, dc in next 2 ch, dc in next dc, ch 2, sk 2 dc, [dc in next dc, ch 2] 3 times, dc in each dc to end. (44 dc in body, 7 dc and 5 ch-sps in lace edging)

Row 84: Ch 2, turn, dc in first dc and in each dc to first ch-2 sp, [ch 2, dc in next dc]

4 times, ch 2, sk 2 dc, dc in next dc, 3 dc in end loop. (44 dc in body, 8 dc and 5 ch-sps in lace edging)

Row 85: Ch 9, turn, dc in 7th ch from hook, dc in next 2 ch, dc in next dc, ch 2, sk 2 dc, [dc in next dc, ch 2] 5 times, dc in each dc to end. (44 dc in body, 9 dc and 7 ch-sps in lace edging)

Row 86: Ch 2, turn, dc in first dc and in each dc to first ch-2 sp, [ch 2, dc in next dc] 5 times, 2 dc in next ch-2 sp, dc in next dc; leave remaining sts unworked. (44 dc in body, 8 dc and 5 ch-sps in lace edging)

Row 87: Ch 5, sk first 3 dc, dc in next dc, 2 dc in next ch-2 sp, [dc in next dc, ch 2] 4 times, dc in each dc to end. (44 dc in body, 7 dc and 5 ch-sps in lace edging)

Row 88: Ch 2, turn, dc in first dc and in each dc to first ch-2 sp, [ch 2, dc in next dc] 3 times, 2 dc in next ch-2 sp, dc in next dc; leave remaining sts unworked. (44 dc in body, 6 dc and 3 ch-sps in lace edging)

Row 89: Ch 5, sk first 3 dc, dc in next dc, 2 dc in next ch-2 sp, [dc in next dc, ch 2] twice, dc in each dc to end. (44 dc in body, 5 dc and 3 ch-sps in lace edging)

Rows 90–105: Rep rows 82–89 twice.

Decrease Section

Row 106: Ch 2, turn, dc in first dc and in each dc to 3 dc before first ch-2 sp, dc2tog, dc in next dc, ch 2, [dc in next dc, ch 2] twice, sk 2 dc, dc in next dc, 3 dc in end ch-sp. (43 dc in body, 6 dc and 3 ch-sps in lace edging)

Row 107: Ch 9, turn, dc in 7th ch from hook, dc in next 2 ch, dc in next dc, ch 2, sk 2 dc, [dc in next dc, ch 2] 3 times, dc in each dc to end. (43 dc in body, 7 dc and 5 ch-sps in lace edging)

Row 108: Ch 2, turn, dc in first dc and in each dc to 3 dc before first ch-2 sp, dc2tog, dc in next dc, [ch 2, dc in next dc] 4 times, ch 2, sk 2 dc, dc in next dc, 3 dc in end ch-sp. (42 dc in body, 8 dc and 5 ch-sps in lace edging)

Row 109: Ch 9, turn, dc in 7th ch from hook, dc in next 2 ch, dc in next dc, ch 2, sk 2 dc, [dc in next dc, ch 2] 5 times, dc in each dc to end. (42 dc in body, 9 dc and 7 ch-sps in lace edging)

Row 110: Ch 2, turn, dc in first dc and in each dc to 3 dc before first ch-2 sp, dc2tog, dc in next dc, [ch 2, dc in next dc] 5 times, 2 dc in next ch-2 sp, dc in next dc; leave remaining sts unworked. (41 dc in body, 8 dc and 5 ch-sps in lace edging)

Row 111: Ch 5, sk first 3 dc, dc in next dc, 2 dc in next ch-2 sp, [dc in next dc, ch 2] 4 times, dc in each dc to end. (41 dc in body, 7 dc and 5 ch-sps in lace edging)

Row 112: Ch 2, turn, dc in first dc and in each dc to 3 dc before first ch-2 sp, dc2tog, dc in next dc, [ch 2, dc in next dc] 3 times, 2 dc in next ch-2 sp, dc in next dc; leave remaining sts unworked. (40 dc in body, 6 dc and 3 ch-sps in lace edging)

Row 113: Ch 5, sk first 3 dc, dc in next dc, 2 dc in next ch-2 sp, [dc in next dc, ch 2] twice, dc in each dc to end. (40 dc in body, 5 dc and 3 ch-sps in lace edging)

Rows 114–185: Rep rows 106–113 nine times. (4 dc in body, 5 dc and 3 ch-sps in lace edging) in row 185.

Fasten off.

Finishing

Weave in all ends. Block to size.

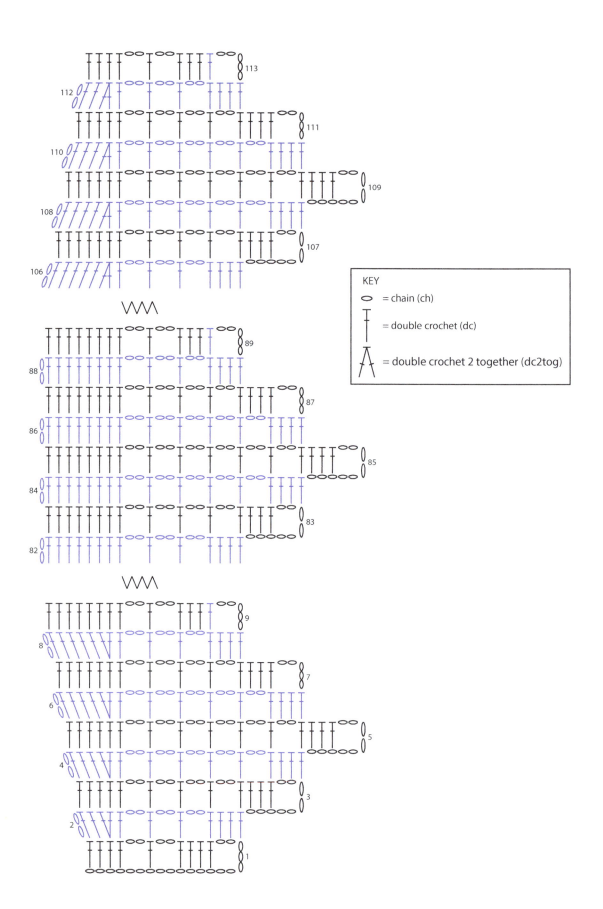

A beautiful garden is not necessarily manicured to perfection. Hidden features such as angles and slopes can bring out the best in a garden – and our Aslant shawl. Worked from one small corner and increasing until the shawl is the needed size, the hidden angles give this simple stitch a very elegant feel.

Skill Level

Intermediate

Finished Size

60 inches (152.5 cm) wide by 34 inches (86 cm) deep blocked

Materials

1300 yards (1189 m) 2-ply fingering weight yarn

Model uses Round Table Yarns Guenevere (100% superwash merino; 100g / 3.5 oz = 398 m / 425 yds) in the colorway "My beauty will not hold"

US size 7 (4.5 mm) crochet hook or size needed for gauge

Yarn needle

Gauge

In main body pattern, 5 stitch repeats and 10 rows = 4 inches when blocked

Special Stitches

Fan: ([dc, ch 2] 3 times, dc) in designated stitch.

V-st: (dc, ch 3, dc) in designated stitch.

Large Fan: ([dc, ch 4] 3 times, dc) in designated space.

Pattern Notes

This pattern only increases on one side of the fabric. This gives the shawl the asymmetrical look.

Once the body is complete, the increased edge becomes the top of the shawl. The remaining two sides become the bottom edge that have the edging applied to it.

Directions

Ch 4.

Body

Row 1 (RS): 4 dc in 4th ch from hook.

Row 2: Ch 1, turn, sc in first dc, ch 3, sk 3 dc, sc in sp between last dc and turning ch, ch 3, sc in top of turning ch. (2 ch-3 sps)

Row 3: Ch 3, turn, *3 dc in next ch-3 sp, ch 1; rep from * across, ending with 3 dc in last ch-3 sp, dc in last dc. (Two 3-dc groups)

Row 4: Ch 1, turn, sc in first dc, * ch 3, sc in next ch- sp, rep from * ending with ch 3, sc in sp between last dc and turning ch, ch 3, sc in top of turning ch. (3 ch-3 sps)

Row 5: Ch 3, turn, *3 dc in next ch-3 sp, ch 1; rep from * across, ending with 3 dc in last ch-3 sp, dc in last sc. (Three 3-dc groups)

Rows 6–107: Rep rows 4 and 5 fifty-one times more. (Row 107 has fifty-four 3dc groups)

Edging

Row 1: Ch 1, turn, sc in first dc, * ch 2, sc in next ch-sp, rep from * ending with ch 2, sc in top of turning ch. (54 ch-2 loops)

Row 2: Ch 1, turn, evenly space 161 sc along sc and ch-2 sps to end of the row making sure the last sc is in the last sc of the row (mark this stitch), working down the sides of the rows, space evenly 160 more sc making sure that the last sc is in the same ch of the beg ch-4 that the first 4 dc of row 1 were worked into. (321 sc)

Row 3: Ch 6, turn, dc in first sc (counts as the first V-st of row); *sk next 4 sc, fan in next sc, sk next 4 sc, V-st in next sc; rep from * across. (32 Fans, 33 V-sts)

Note: Marked stitch in row 2 should have a V-st in it.

Row 4: Turn, sl st in next ch-3 sp, ch 1, sc in same sp; *ch 3, large fan in center ch-2 sp of next fan, ch 3, sc in ch-3 sp of next V-st; rep from * to end. Fasten off.

Finishing

Weave in all ends. Block to dimensions.

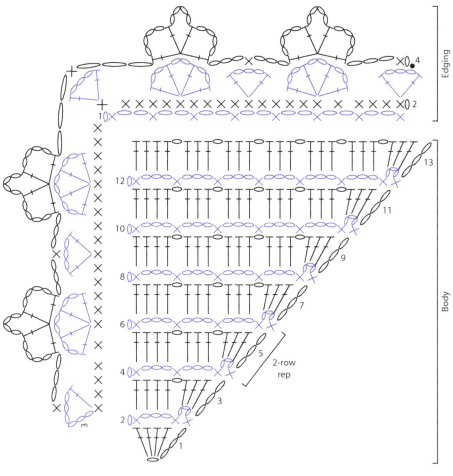

KEY

● = slip stitch (sl st)

○ = chain (ch)

✕ = single crochet (sc)

T = double crochet (dc)

= Fan

= V-st

= Large Fan

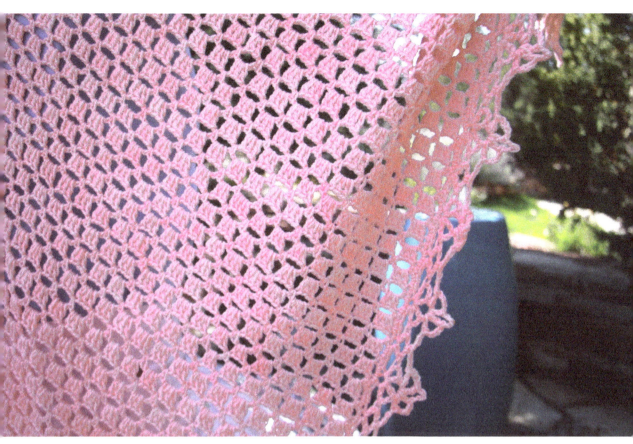

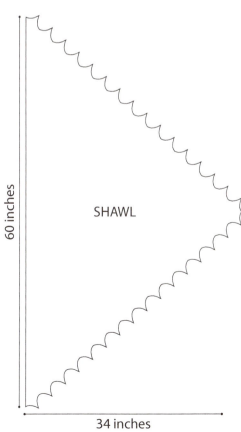

SHAWL

60 inches

34 inches

Solar

Sunshine. Our beautiful garden cannot thrive without the sun's rays washing everything with life-giving warmth and light. Solar evokes that wonderful feeling in a top-down shawl that grows with rays of gently changing color. Wrap yourself up in sunshine any time of the year.

Skill Level

Intermediate

Finished Size

48 inches (122 cm) wide by 24 inches (61 cm) deep at longest point, blocked

Materials

675 yards (617 m) fingering weight yarn

Model uses Black Trillium Fibres Lilt Sock Gradient Kit (85% superwash merino / 15% silk; 5.8 oz / 165 g = 675 yds / 617 m) in the colorway Squash Blossom

US size E/4 (3.5mm) crochet hook or size needed for gauge

5 stitch markers
Yarn needle

Gauge

20 dc and 8 dc rows = 4 inches (10 cm) when blocked

Special Stitches

FPdc: Front-post double crochet—Yarn over, insert hook from front to back and then to front again around post of stitch, yarn over and draw up loop, [yarn over and draw through 2 loops on hook] twice.

BPdc: Back-post double crochet—Yarn over, insert hook from back to front and then to back again around post of stitch, yarn over and draw up loop, [yarn over and draw through 2 loops on hook] twice.

Shell: (2 dc, ch 2, 2 dc) in indicated stitch or space.

Pattern Notes

The Ch-2 at the beginning of each row DOES NOT count as a stitch

When winding a gradient yarn that comes in separate skeins like this one, I used the Russian Join technique so that all of the colors were ready to go in one skein. Here is a really great tutorial: www.craftsy.com/blog/2015/12/russian-join

Directions

Ch 3.

Row 1: 6 dc in 3rd ch from hook. (6 dc)

Row 2: Ch 2, turn; 2 dc in each dc. (12 dc)

Row 3: Ch 2, turn; 2 dc in next dc, dc in next dc; [FPdc around next dc, dc in same dc, dc in next dc] 5 times. (18 dc)

Row 4: Ch 2, turn; 2 dc in next dc, dc in next dc; [BPdc around next FPdc, dc in same dc, dc in each of next 2 dc] 5 times, dc in last dc. (24 dc)

Row 5: Ch 2, turn; 2 dc in next dc, [dc in each dc to next BPdc; FPdc around next BPdc, dc in same BPdc] 5 times, dc in each dc to end. (30 sts)

Row 6: Ch 2, turn; 2 dc in next dc, [dc in each dc to next FPdc; BPdc around next FPdc, dc in same FPdc] 5 times, dc in each dc to end. (36 sts)

Rows 7–20: Rep rows 5 and 6 seven times. (120 sts)

Row 21: Ch 2, turn; 2 dc in next dc, dc in next 8 dc, shell in next dc, dc in next 10 dc, [FPdc around next BPdc, dc in same BPdc, dc in next 8 dc, shell in next dc, dc in next 10 dc] 5 times. (144 dc)

Row 22: Ch 2, turn; sk 1st dc, dc in each dc to next ch-2 sp, shell in ch-2 sp, [dc in next 11 dc, sk 2 dc, dc in next dc and place a marker in the dc just made, dc in each dc to next ch-2 sp, shell in ch-2 sp] 5 times, dc in next 10 dc, sk next dc, dc in last dc. (156 sts; 26 sts between ch-2 sps)

Row 23: Ch 2, turn; sk 1st dc, dc in each dc to next ch-2 sp, shell in next ch-2 sp, [dc in each dc to marked dc, sk the marked dc and the next dc, dc in next dc and move marker to dc just made, dc in each dc to next ch-2 sp, shell in ch-2 sp] 5 times, dc in each dc to last 2 dc, sk next dc, dc in last dc. (168 sts; 28 sts between ch-2 sps)

Row 24: Ch 2, turn, sk 1st dc, dc in next dc, (ch 1, sk next dc, dc in next dc) to next ch-2 sp, ch 1, (dc, ch 2, dc) in ch-2 sp, ch 1, dc in next dc, *(ch 1, sk next dc, dc in next dc) to marker, sk 2 dc, dc in next dc and move marker to dc just made, (ch 1, sk next dc, dc in next dc) to next ch-2 sp, ch 1, (dc, ch 2, dc) in next ch-2 sp, ch 1, dc in next dc; rep from * 4 more times, (ch 1, sk next dc, dc in next dc) to last 3 dc, ch 1, sk 2 dc, dc in last dc. (14 ch-1 sps between ch-2 sps)

Row 25: Ch 2, turn; sk 1st dc, dc in each dc and ch-1 sp to next ch-2 sp, shell in next ch-2 sp, *dc in each dc and ch-1 sp to marker, sk 2 dc, dc in next dc and move marker to dc just made, dc in each dc and ch-1 sp to next ch-2 sp, shell in ch-2 sp; rep from * 4 more times, dc in each dc and ch-1 sp to last ch-1 sp, sk ch-1 sp, dc in last dc. (192 sts; 32 sts between ch-2 sps)

Rows 26–29: Repeat Row 23 four times. (240 sts; 40 sts between ch-2 sps)

Rows 30–35: Repeat Rows 24–29. (312 sts; 52 sts between ch-2 sps)

Rows 36 and 37: Repeat Rows 24 and 25. (336 sts; 56 sts between ch-2 sps)

Rows 38 and 39: Repeat Row 23 twice. (360 sts; 60 sts between ch-2 sps)

Rows 40–43: Repeat Rows 36–39. (408 sts; 68 sts between ch-2 sps)

Rows 44–47: Repeat Rows 24 and 25 twice. (456 sts; 76 sts between ch-2 sps)

Row 48: Repeat Row 24. (468 sts; 38 ch-1 sps between ch-2 sps).

Fasten off.

Finishing

Weave in all ends. Block to size and shape.

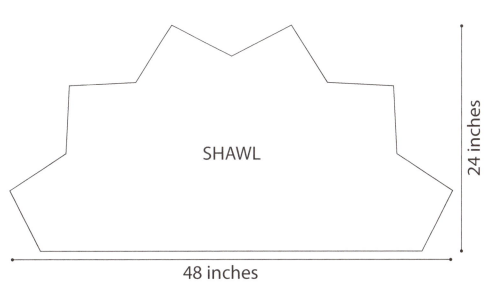

SHAWL

24 inches

48 inches

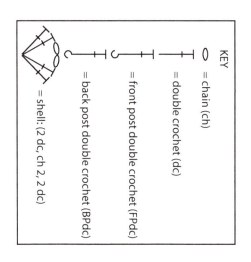

KEY

O = chain (ch)

= double crochet (dc)

= front post double crochet (FPdc)

= back post double crochet (BPdc)

= shell: (2 dc, ch 2, 2 dc)

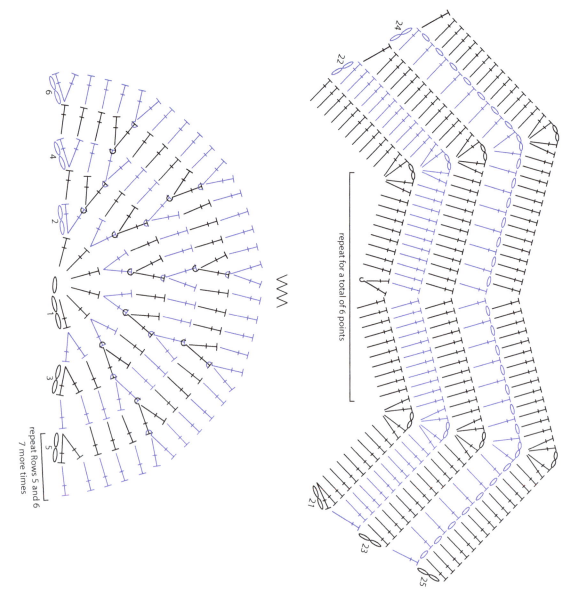

repeat Rows 5 and 6
7 more times

repeat for a total of 6 points

Ecliptic

Every few months it happens: the covering of the sun with the moon. When the eclipse happens, the world and the wash of light as we know it changes. Ecliptic gives us a different view of a sun smothered with a bit of darkness. Worked from the top down the rays are tamed in a more triangular shape that envelops you day or night.

Skill Level

Intermediate

Finished Size

52 inches (132 cm) wide by 26 inches (66 cm) deep at longest point

Materials

750 yards (686 m) laceweight yarn

Model is shown in Anzula Luxury Fibers Breeze (65% silk / 35% linen; 750 yds / 686 m = 4 oz / 113g) in the colorway Persimmon

Size 3.0 mm crochet hook or size needed for gauge

Stitch marker
Yarn needle

Gauge

20 tr and 5.5 patt rows = 4 inches (10 cm) when blocked

Special Stitches

Shell: (3 tr, ch 2, 3 tr) in space indicated.

V-st: (Tr, ch 1, tr) in stitch or space indicated.

Dbl-v: (2 tr, ch 1, 2 tr) in space indicated

Fan: (Tr, [ch 1, tr] 6 times) in space indicated.

Pattern Notes

Placing a stitch marker in the center Shell of the shawl helps with stitch placement. Move marker up with each row.

The length and width of the shawl are just a guideline. You can increase the length and width of the shawl by repeating rows 11–14 more times. You may require more yarn in this case.

Directions

Row 1: Ch 6, tr in 6th ch from hook (beginning ch and first tr count as first V-st), ch 1, Shell in same ch, ch 1, V-st in same ch. (1 Shell, 2 V-st)

Row 2: Ch 5, turn, tr in 1st tr (beginning ch and following tr count as first V-st here and throughout); ch 1, sk first ch-1 sp, tr in next ch-1 sp, tr in next 3 tr, (tr, ch 1, Shell, ch 1, tr) in next ch-2 sp, tr in next 3 tr, tr in next ch-1 sp, ch 1, V-st in 4th ch of beg ch. (10 tr, 2 V-st, 1 Shell)

NOTE: Shell just completed is center Shell. If using stitch marker to help with placement of stitches, put marker in this Shell.

Row 3: Ch 5, turn, tr in 1st tr, sk first ch-1 sp; *ch 1, tr in next ch-1 sp, tr in next 2 tr, V-st in next tr, tr in next 2 tr, tr in next ch-1 sp, ch 1;* Shell in next ch-2 sp; rep from * to * once more, V-st in 4th ch of beg ch. (12 tr, 4 V-st, 1 Shell)

Row 4: Ch 5, turn, tr in 1st tr; sk first ch-1 sp; *ch 1, tr in next ch-1 sp, tr in next 3 tr, ch 1, sk next tr, V-st in next ch-1 sp, ch 1, sk next tr, tr in next 3 tr, tr in next ch-1 sp, ch 1;* Shell in next ch-2 sp; rep from * to * once more, V-st in 4th ch of beg ch. (16 tr, 4 V-st, 1 Shell)

Rows 5 and 6: Ch 5, turn, tr in 1st tr; sk first ch-1 sp; *ch 1, tr in next ch-1 sp, tr in each tr across to next ch-1 sp, ch 1, sk next ch-1 sp, Dbl-v in next ch-1 sp, ch 1, sk next ch-1 sp, tr in each tr across to next ch-1 sp, tr in next ch-1 sp, ch 1;* Shell in next ch-2 sp; rep from * to * once more, V-st in 4th ch of beg ch. (24 tr, 2 V-st, 2 Dbl-v, 1 Shell) at end of Row 6.

Row 7: Ch 5, turn, tr in 1st tr, sk first ch-1 sp; *ch 1, tr in next ch-1 sp, tr in next 2 tr, V-st in next tr, tr in next 3 tr, ch 1, sk next ch-1 sp, Shell in next ch-1 sp, ch 1, sk next ch-1 sp, tr in next 3 tr, V-st in next tr, tr in next 2 tr, tr in next ch-1 sp, ch 1;* Shell in next ch-2 sp; rep from * to * once more, V-st in 4th ch of beg ch. (6 V-st, 3 Shells)

Row 8: Ch 5, turn, tr in 1st tr, sk first ch-1 sp; *ch 1, tr in next ch-1 sp, tr in next 3 tr, ch 1, sk next tr, V-st in next ch-1 sp, ch 1, sk next tr, tr in next 3 tr, ch 1, sk next ch-1 sp, Shell in next ch-2 sp, ch 1, sk next ch-1 sp, tr in next 3 tr, ch 1, sk next tr, V-st in next ch-1 sp, ch 1, sk next tr, tr in next 3 tr, tr in next ch-1 sp, ch 1;* Shell in next ch-2 sp; rep from * to * once more, V-st in 4th ch of beg ch.

Rows 9 and 10: Ch 5, turn, tr in 1st tr, sk first ch-1 sp; *ch 1, tr in next ch-1 sp, tr in each tr across to next ch-1 sp, ch 1, sk next ch-1 sp, Dbl-v in next ch-1 sp, ch 1, sk next ch-1 sp, tr in next 3 tr, ch 1, sk next ch-1 sp, Shell in next ch-2 sp, ch 1, sk next ch-1 sp, tr in next 3 tr, ch 1, sk next ch-1 sp, Dbl-v in next ch-1 sp, ch 1, sk next ch-1 sp, tr in each tr across to next ch-1 sp, tr in next ch-1 sp, ch 1;* Shell in next ch-2 sp; rep from * to * once more, V-st in 4th ch of beg ch. (2 V-sts, 4 Dbl-v, 3 Shells)

Row 11: Ch 5, turn, tr in 1st tr, sk first ch-1 sp; ch 1, tr in next ch-1 sp, tr in next 2 tr, V-st in next tr, tr in next 3 tr, *ch 1, sk next ch-1 sp, Shell in next ch-sp, ch 1, sk next ch-1 sp, tr in next 3 tr; rep from * across to 3 tr before center Shell , V-st in next tr, tr in next 2 tr, tr in next ch-1 sp, ch 1, Shell in next ch-2 sp, ch 1, tr in next ch-1 sp, tr in next 2 tr, V-st in next tr, tr in next 3 tr, **ch 1, sk next ch-1 sp, Shell in next ch-sp, ch 1, sk next ch-1 sp, tr in next 3 tr; rep from ** across to 3 tr before last V-st, V-st in next tr, tr in next 2 tr, tr in next ch-1 sp, ch 1, V-st in 4th ch of beg ch. (6 V-st, 7 Shells)

Row 12: Ch 5, turn, tr in 1st tr, sk first ch-1 sp; ch 1, tr in next ch-1 sp, tr in next 3 tr, ch 1, sk next tr, V-st in next ch-1 sp, ch 1, sk next tr, tr in next 3 tr, *ch 1, sk next ch-1 sp, Shell in next ch-2 sp, ch 1, sk next ch-1 sp, tr in next 3 tr ;rep from * across to V-st before center Shell, ch, 1, sk next tr, V-st in next ch-1 sp, ch 1, sk next tr, tr in next 3 tr, tr in next ch-1 sp, ch 1, Shell in next ch-2 sp, ch 1, tr in next ch-1 sp, tr in next 3 tr, ch 1, sk next tr, V-st in next ch-1 sp, ch 1, sk next tr, tr in next 3 tr, **ch 1, sk next ch-1 sp, Shell in next ch-2 sp, ch 1, sk next ch-1 sp, tr in next 3 tr; rep from ** across to last 2 V-sts, ch 1, sk next tr, V-st in next ch-1 sp, ch 1, sk next tr, tr in next 3 tr, tr in next ch-1 sp, ch 1, V-st in 4th ch of beg ch.

Rows 13 and 14: Ch 5, turn, tr in 1st tr, sk first ch-1 sp; ch 1, tr in next ch-1 sp, tr in each tr across to next ch-1 sp, ch 1, sk next ch-1 sp, Dbl-v in next ch-1 sp, ch 1, sk next ch-1 sp, tr in next 3 tr, *ch 1, sk next ch-1 sp, Shell in next ch-2 sp, ch 1, sk next ch-1 sp, tr in next 3 tr; rep

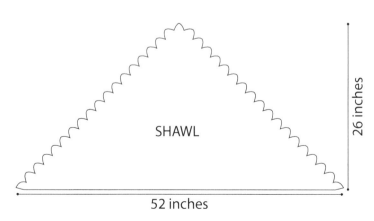

SHAWL

26 inches

52 inches

from * across to 4 ch-1 sps before center Shell , ch, 1, sk next ch-1 sp, Dbl-v in next ch-1 sp, ch 1, sk next ch-1 sp, tr in each tr across to next ch-1 sp, tr in next ch-1 sp, ch 1, Shell in next ch-2 sp, ch 1, tr in next ch-1 sp, tr in each tr across to next ch-1 sp, ch 1, sk next ch-1 sp, Dbl-v in next ch-1 sp, ch 1, sk next ch-1 sp, tr in next 3 tr, **ch 1, sk next ch-1 sp, Shell in next ch-2 sp, ch 1, sk next ch-1 sp, tr in next 3 tr; rep from ** across to 4 ch-1 sps before beginning ch, ch 1, sk next ch-1 sp, Dbl-v in next ch-1 sp, ch 1, sk next ch-1 sp, tr in each tr across to next ch-1 sp, tr in next ch-1 sp, ch 1,

V-st in 4th ch of beg ch; ch 5, turn. (2 V-st, 4 Dbl-v, 7 Shells)

Rows 15–38: Work Rows 11–14 six more times.

Edging

Row 1: Ch 5, turn, tr in 1st tr, ch 2, sk next ch-1 sp, sk next 3 tr, sc in sp between last skipped tr and next tr, ch 2, Fan in ch-sp of next Dbl-v, ch 2, sk next ch-1 sp, sc in center tr of next 3-tr group, *ch 2, Fan in ch-2 sp of next Shell, ch 2, sk next ch-1 sp, sc in center tr of next 3-tr group;* rep between * and * across to Dbl-v before center shell, ch 2, Fan in ch-sp of next Dbl-v, ch 2, sk next 3 tr, sc in

sp between last skipped tr and next tr, ch 2, [(tr, ch 1) 8 times, tr] in ch-2 sp of center Shell; ch 2, sk next 3 tr, sc in sp between last skipped tr and next tr, ch 2, Fan in ch-sp of next Dbl-v, ch 2, sk next ch-1 sp, sc in center tr of next 3-tr group, rep between * and * across to next Dbl-v; ch 2, Fan in ch-sp of next Dbl-v, ch 2, sk next ch-1 sp, sc in center tr of next 3-tr group, rep between * and * across to next Dbl-v; ch 2, Fan in ch-sp of next Dbl-v, ch 2, sk next 3 tr, sc in sp between last skipped tr and next tr, ch 2, V-st in 4th ch of beg ch. Fasten off.

Finishing

Weave in ends. Lightly block to size.

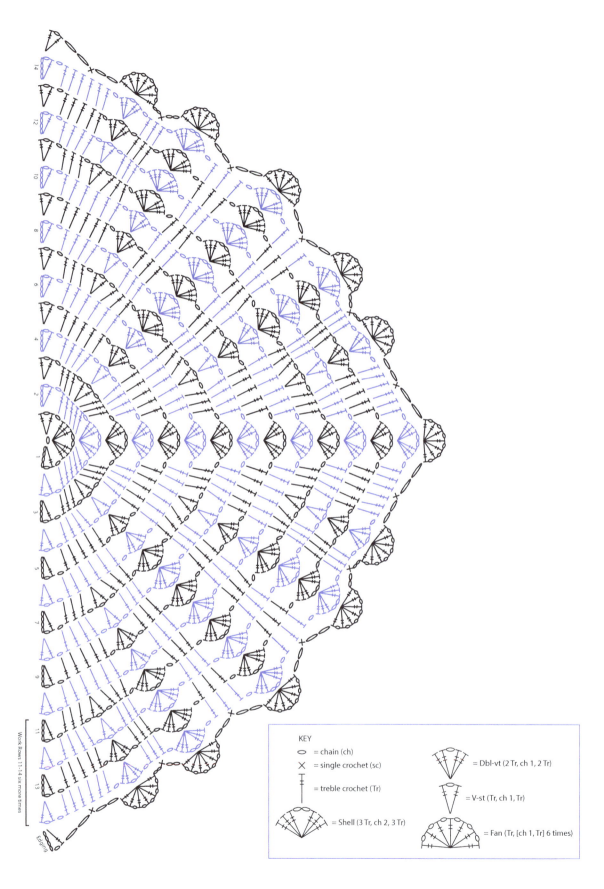

KEY

◯ = chain (ch)

✕ = single crochet (sc)

| = treble crochet (Tr)

= Shell (3 Tr, ch 2, 3 Tr)

= Dbl-vt (2 Tr, ch 1, 2 Tr)

= V-st (Tr, ch 1, Tr)

= Fan (Tr, [ch 1, Tr] 6 times)

Work Rows 11–14 six more times

Edging

Breeze

Imagine walking through your garden with just a dainty caress of a summer breeze on your arms. It tempers the heat of the day, making your stroll even more lovely. Breeze is worked from side to side in a soft lace weight yarn and will feel like a soft summer chinook on the most elegant of nights.

Skill Level

Intermediate

Finished Size

66 inches (168 cm) wide by 14 inches (36 cm) deep

Materials

700 yds (823 m) laceweight yarn

Model uses Blue Moon Fiber Arts Laci (100% extrafine 80's merino; 900 yds / 822 m = 4 oz / 118g) in the colorway Midsummers Night

Size 3.0 mm crochet hook or size needed for gauge

Yarn needle

Gauge

24 dc and 12 dc rows = 4 inches (10 cm) when blocked

Special Stitches

Shell: (3 dc, ch 2, 3 dc) in stitch indicated

dc2tog: Double crochet 2 together – [Yarn over, insert hook in next st and draw up a loop, yarn over and draw through 2 loops on hook] twice, yarn over and draw through all 3 loops on hook.

Pattern Notes

The ch-2 at the plainfield side of work does not count as a stitch. You will work your first Double crochet in the very first stitch instead of skipping.

Directions

Ch 19.

Increase section

Row 1: Shell in in 6th ch from hook, ch 5, sk next 4 ch, shell in next ch (for lace edge section of shawl), ch 2, sk next 3 ch, dc in next ch, ch 1 (for divider between lace edge and plainfield),, sk next ch, dc in each of last 3 dc (for plainfield section of shawl), ch 2, turn. (2 shells, 1 ch-5 sp and a beginning ch-5 sp in lace edge; 3 dc in plainfield)

Row 2: Dc in first dc, 2 dc in next dc, dc in next dc, ch 1, sk next ch-1 sp, dc in next dc, ch 2, shell in ch-2 sp of next shell, ch 2, sc in 3rd ch of next ch-5 sp, ch 2, shell in ch-2 sp of next shell, ch 2, dc in 3rd ch of ch-5 turning ch, ch 5, turn. (2 shells, 3 ch-2 sps,and ending dc in lace edge; 4 dc in plainfield)

Row 3: Dc in first dc of first shell, ch 2, shell in ch-2 sp of same shell, ch 3, sk next ch-2 sp, sc in next sc, ch 3, sk next ch-2 sp, shell in ch-2 sp of next shell, ch 2, sk next ch-2 sp, dc in next dc, ch 1, sk next ch-1 sp, dc in each dc to end, ch 2, turn. (2 shells, 2 ch-3 sps, 1 ch-2 sp, 1 separate dc and a beginning ch-5 sp in lace edge; 4 dc in plainfield)

Row 4: Dc in first dc and in each dc to last 2 dc before next ch-1 sp, 2 dc in next dc, dc in next dc, ch 1, sk next ch-1 sp, dc in next dc, ch 2, sk next ch-2 sp, shell in ch-2 sp of next shell, ch 5, sk next 2 ch-3 sps, shell in ch-2 sp of next shell, ch 2, dc in last dc of same shell, 2 dc in next ch-2 sp, dc in next dc, 3 dc in turning ch-sp, dc in 3rd ch of ch-5 turning ch, ch 3, turn. (2 shells, 1 ch-5 sp, 1 ch-2 sp and 8 ending dc in lace edge; 5 dc in plainfield)

Row 5: Sk first dc, dc in each of next 7 dc, ch 2, sk next ch-2 sp, dc in first dc of next shell, ch 2, shell in ch-2 sp same shell, ch 2, sc in 3rd ch of next ch-5 sp, ch 2, shell in ch-2 sp of next shell, ch 2, sk next ch-2 sp, dc in next dc, ch 1, sk next ch-1 sp, dc in each dc to end, ch 2, turn. (2 shells, 4 ch-2 sps, 7 beginning dc and 1 beginning

14 inches

66 inches

SHAWL

ch-3 in lace edge; 5 dc in plainfield)

Row 6: Dc in first dc and in each dc to last 2 dc before next ch-1 sp, 2 dc in next dc, dc in next dc, ch 1, sk next ch-1 sp, dc in next dc, ch 2, sk next ch-2 sp, shell in ch-2 sp of next shell, ch 3, sk next ch-2 sp, sc in next sc, ch 3, sk next ch-2 sp, shell in ch-2 sp of next shell, ch 2, dc in last dc of same shell, (ch 2, sk next ch-2 sp, dc in next dc) twice, (ch 2, sk next 2 dc, dc in next dc) twice, ch 5 (for corner), dc in top of turning ch, working along side of edging, ch 2, dc in base of same turning ch, ch 2, dc in base of next dc, ch 2, dc in base of next turning ch, ch 2, sk dc at end of next row, sl st in beginning ch-sp of Row 1, ch 1, turn. (2 shells, 2 ch-3 sps, 5 ch-2 sps, 1 corner ch-5 sp in lace edging; 4 ch-2 sps in side edging; 6 dc in plainfield)

Row 7: Working along side edge, sc in next sl st, (ch 3, 2 sc in next ch-2 sp) 4 times; working in corner, (ch 3, 2 sc, ch 3, 3 sc, ch 3, 2 sc) in next ch-5 sp; working along lace edge, (ch 3, 2 sc in next ch-2 sp) 5 times, ch 3, shell in ch-2 sp of next shell, ch 5, sk next 2 ch-3 sps, shell in ch-2 sp of next shell, ch 2, sk ch-2 sp, dc in next dc, ch 1, sk next ch-1 sp, dc in each dc to end, ch 2, turn. (2 shells, 1 ch-5 sp, 6 ch-3 sps in lace edge; 4 ch-3 sps in side edging; 6 dc in plainfield)

Row 8: Dc in first dc and in each dc to last 2 dc before next ch-1 sp, 2 dc in next dc, dc in next dc, ch 1, sk next ch-1 sp, dc in next dc, ch 2, sk next ch-2 sp, shell in ch-2 sp of next shell,, ch 2, sc in 3rd ch of next ch-5 sp, ch 2, shell in ch-2 sp of next shell, ch 2, dc in next ch-3 sp, leave remaining sts unworked, ch 5, turn. (2 shells, 3 ch-2 sps, and ending dc in lace edge; 7 dc in plainfield)

Rows 9–11: Repeat rows 3–5. (8 dc in plainfield)

Row 12: Work same as row 6, working last sl st in ch-3 sp before shell in next row, ch 1, turn. (9 dc in plainfield)

Row 13: Repeat row 7.

Rows 14–91: Repeat rows 8–13 thirteen more times. (48 dc in plainfield)

Center section

Row 92: Dc in first dc and in each dc to next ch-1 sp, ch 1, sk next ch-1 sp, dc in next dc, ch 2, sk next ch-2 sp, shell in ch-2 sp of next shell, ch 2, sc in 3rd ch of next ch-5 sp, ch 2, shell in ch-2 sp of next shell, ch 2, dc in next ch-3 sp, leave remaining sts unworked, ch 5, turn.

Row 93: Dc in first dc of next shell, ch 2, shell in ch-2 sp of next shell, ch 3, sk next ch-2 sp, sc in next sc, ch 3, sk next ch-2 sp, shell inch-2 sp of next shell, ch 2, sk next ch-2 sp, dc in next dc, ch 1, sk next ch-2 sp, dc in each dc to end, ch 2, turn.

Row 94: Dc in first dc and in each dc to next ch-1 sp, ch 1, sk next ch-1 sp, dc in next dc, ch 2, sk next ch-2 sp, shell in ch-2 sp of next shell, ch 5, sk next 2 ch-3 sps, shell in ch-2 sp of next shell, ch 2, dc in last dc of same shell, 2 dc in next ch-2 sp, dc in next dc, 3 dc in turning ch-sp, dc in 3rd ch of ch-5 turning ch, ch 3, turn.

Row 95: Sk first dc, dc in each of next 7 dc, ch 2, sk next ch-2 sp, dc in first dc of next shell, ch 2, shell in ch-2 sp of same shell, ch 2, sc in 3rd ch of next ch-5 sp, ch 2, shell in ch-2 sp of next shell, ch 2, sk next ch-2 sp, dc in next dc, ch 1, sk next ch-1 sp, dc in each dc to end, ch 2, turn.

Row 96: Dc in first dc and in each dc to next ch-1 sp, ch 1, sk next ch-1 sp, dc in next dc, ch 2, sk next ch-2 sp, shell in ch-2 sp of next shell, ch 3, sk next ch-2 sp, sc in next sc, ch 3, sk next ch-2 sp, shell in ch-2 sp of next shell, ch 2, dc in last dc of same shell, (ch 2, sk next ch-2 sp, dc in next dc) twice, (ch 2, sk next 2 dc, dc in next dc) twice, ch 5, dc in top of turning ch; working along side of edging, ch 2, dc in base of same turning ch, ch 2, dc in base of next dc, ch 2, dc in base of next turning ch, ch 2, sk dc at end of next row, sl st in ch-3 sp before shell in next row, ch 1, turn.

Row 97: Working along side edge, sc in next sl st, (ch 3, 2 sc

in next ch-2 sp) 4 times; working in corner, (ch 3, 2 sc, ch 3, 3 sc, ch 3, 2 sc) in next ch-5 sp; working along lace edge, (ch 3, 2 sc in next ch-2 sp) 5 times, ch 3, shell in ch-2 sp of next shell, ch 5, sk next 2 ch-3 sps, shell in ch-2 sp of next shell, ch 2, sk ch-2 sp, dc in next dc, ch 1, sk next ch-1 sp, dc in each dc to end, ch 2, turn.

Rows 98–109: Repeat rows 92–97 twice more.

Decrease section

Row 110: Dc in first dc and in each dc to last 3 dc before next ch-1 sp, dc2tog, dc in next dc, ch 1, sk next ch-1 sp, dc in next dc, ch 2, sk next ch-2 sp, shell in ch-2 sp of next shell,, ch 2, sc in 3rd ch of next ch-5 sp, ch 2, shell in ch-2 sp of next shell, ch 2, dc in next ch-3 sp, leave remaining sts unworked, ch 5, turn. (47 dc in plainfield)

Row 111: Dc in first dc of next shell, ch 2, shell in ch-2 sp of next shell, ch 3, sk next ch-2 sp, sc in next sc, ch 3, sk next ch-2 sp, shell in ch-2 sp of next shell, ch 2, sk next ch-2 sp, dc in next dc, ch 1, sk next ch-2 sp, dc in each dc to end, ch 2, turn.

Row 112: Dc in first dc and in each dc to last 3 dc before next ch-1 sp, dc2tog, dc in next dc, ch 1, sk next ch-1 sp, dc in next dc, ch 2, sk next ch-2 sp, shell in ch-2 sp of next shell, ch 5, sk next 2 ch-3 sps, shell in ch-2 sp of next shell, ch 2, dc in last dc of same shell, 2 dc in next

ch-2 sp, dc in next dc, 3 dc in turning ch-sp, dc in 3rd ch of ch-5 turning ch, ch 3, turn. (46 dc in plainfield)

Row 113: Sk first dc, dc in each of next 7 dc, ch 2, sk next ch-2 sp, dc in first dc of next shell, ch 2, shell in ch-2 sp of same shell, ch 2, sc in 3rd ch of next ch-5 sp, ch 2, shell in ch-2 sp of next shell, ch 2, sk next ch-2 sp, dc in next dc, ch 1, sk next ch-1 sp, dc in each dc to end, ch 2, turn.

Row 114: Dc in first dc and in each dc to last 3 dc before next ch-1 sp, dc2tog, dc in next dc, ch 1, sk next ch-1 sp, dc in next dc, ch 2, sk next ch-2 sp, shell in ch-2 sp of next shell, ch 3, sk next ch-2 sp, sc in next sc, ch 3, sk next ch-2 sp, shell in ch-2 sp of next shell, ch 2, dc in last dc of same shell, (ch 2, sk next ch-2 sp, dc in next dc) twice, (ch 2, sk next 2 dc, dc in next dc) twice, ch 5, dc in top of turning ch; working along side of edging, ch 2, dc in base of same turning ch, ch 2, dc in base of next dc, ch 2, dc in base of next turning ch, ch 2, sk dc at end of next row, sl st in ch-3 sp before shell in next row, ch 1, turn. (45 dc in plainfield)

Row 115: Working along side edge, sc in next sl st, (ch 3, 2 sc in next ch-2 sp) 4 times; working in corner, (ch 3, 2 sc, ch 3, 3 sc, ch 3, 2 sc) in next ch-5 sp; working along lace edge, (ch 3, 2 sc in next ch-2 sp) 5 times, ch 3, shell in ch-2 sp of next shell, ch 5, sk next 2 ch-3 sps, shell in ch-2 sp of next shell, ch 2, sk ch-2 sp, dc in next dc, ch 1, sk next ch-1 sp, dc in each dc to end, ch 2, turn.

Rows 116–198: Repeat Rows 110–115 thirteen times more, then Rows 110 to 114 once more. (4 dc in plainfield)

Row 199: Working along side edge, sc in next sl st, (ch 3, 2 sc in next ch-2 sp) 4 times; working in corner, (ch 3, 2 sc, ch 3, 3 sc, ch 3, 2 sc) in next ch-5 sp; working along lace edge, (ch 3, 2 sc in next ch-2 sp) 5 times, ch 3, sl st in ch-2 sp of next shell, ch 4, sk next 2 ch-3 sps, sl st in ch-2 sp of next shell, ch 2, sk next ch-2 sp, dc in next dc, ch 1, sk next ch-1 sp, dc in each dc to end. Fasten off.

Finishing

Weave in all ends. Wet block to shape, taking care to keep points crisp.

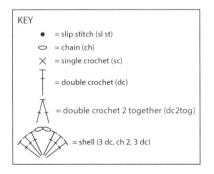

KEY

- ● = slip stitch (sl st)
- ◯ = chain (ch)
- ✕ = single crochet (sc)
- ⊺ = double crochet (dc)
- ⋀ = double crochet 2 together (dc2tog)
- = shell (3 dc, ch 2, 3 dc)

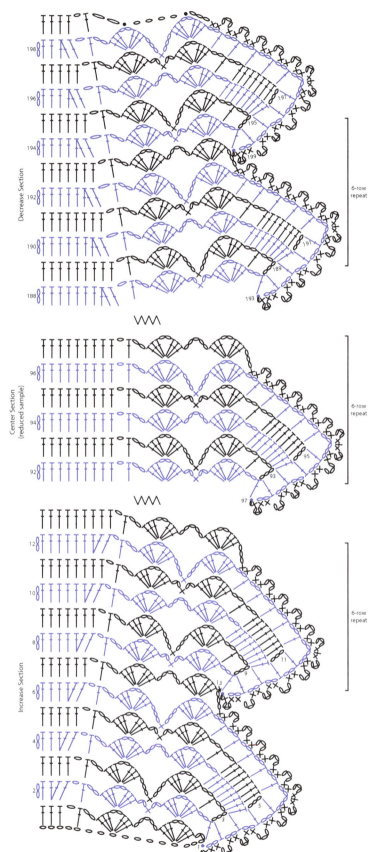

Drift

Magical water – no garden can live without it. Whether it sprinkles down from the sky or pools on the ground soaking our thirsty plants, water is one of a garden's necessities. Drift is no different. This top down shawl with gorgeous texture and shifting colors is a must for your casual wardrobe.

Skill Level

Intermediate

Finished Size

Blocked measurements: 60 inches (152 cm) wing span and 33 inches (84 cm) deep at longest point

Materials

1100 yards (1006 m) laceweight gradient yarn

Model uses YOTH yarns' Mother (100% domestic Rambouillet wool; 3.5 oz / 100g = 550 yds / 503 m) in colorways Spring Water, Blue Raspberry, Blueberry and Caviar (See pattern notes on how this worked.)

US size D/3 (3.25 mm) crochet hook or size needed for gauge

Stitch marker
Yarn needle

Gauge

Approximately 7 shell repeats and 8 rows = 4 inches (10 cm) when blocked

Special Stitches

FPdc: Front-post double crochet – Yarn over, insert hook from front to back and then to front again around post of stitch, yarn over and draw up loop, [yarn over and draw through 2 loops on hook] twice.

BPdc: Back-post double crochet – Yarn over, insert hook from back to front and then to back again around post of stitch, yarn over and draw up loop, [yarn over and draw through 2 loops on hook] twice.

Shell: (2 dc, ch 2, 2 dc) in stitch or space indicated.

Pattern Notes

I wound ½ skein of each colorway together to make the gradient. 1 full skein of each colorway will make 2 shawls.

The ch 3 skipped at the beginning of every row counts as a dc.

You will work in the very first dc of the row every row.

Directions

Ch 4.

Row 1: (3 dc, ch 2, 4 dc) in 4th ch from hook. (8 dc)

NOTE: Place marker in ch-2 sp for future stitch placement. This marks the middle of the shawl. You will move the marker up as you work into this space, always placing the marker in the ch-2 space.

Row 2: Ch 3, turn, dc in first st, ch 1, BPdc (see special stitches) around next st, dc in same st, ch 1, sk 2 dc, shell (see special stitches) in marked space, ch 1, sk 2 dc, dc in next st, BPdc around same st, ch 1, 2 dc in top of beg ch-3. (1 shell; 4 sts and 2 ch-1 sps on each side of center shell)

Row 3: Ch 3, turn, dc in first st, ch 1, sk next ch-1 sp, FPdc (see special stitches) around next st, dc in next dc, FPdc around same st, ch 1, sk next ch-1 sp, shell in marked sp, ch 1, sk next ch-1 sp, FPdc around next st, dc in same st, FPdc around next st, ch 1, 2 dc in top of beg ch-3. (5 sts and 2 ch-1 sps on each side of center shell)

Row 4: Ch 3, turn, dc in first st, [ch 1, sk next ch-1 sp, BPdc around next st, ch 1, shell in next st, ch 1, BPdc around next st, ch 1, sk next ch-1 sp], shell in marked sp; rep between [ ] once, 2 dc in top of beg ch-3. (3 shells)

Row 5: Ch 3, turn, dc in first st, [ch 1, sk next ch-1 sp, FPdc around next st, dc in same st, ch 1, shell in next ch-2 sp, ch 1, sk next ch-1 sp, dc in next st, FPdc around same st, ch 1, sk next ch-1 sp], shell in marked sp; rep between [ ] once, 2 dc in top of beg ch-3.

Row 6: Ch 3, turn, dc in first st, [ch 1, sk next ch-1 sp, BPdc around next st, dc in same st, BPdc around next st, ch 1, sk next ch-1 sp, shell in next ch-2 sp, ch 1, sk next ch-1 sp, BPdc around next st, dc in next st, BPdc around same st, ch 1, sk next ch-1 sp], shell in marked

sp, rep between [ ] once, 2 dc in top of beg ch-3.

Row 7: Ch 3, turn, dc in first st, *ch 1, sk next ch-1 sp, FPdc around next st, ch 1, shell in next st, ch 1, FPdc around next st, ch 1, sk next ch-1 sp, shell in next ch-2 sp; rep from * twice more, ch 1, sk next ch-1 sp, FPdc around next st, ch 1, shell in next st, ch 1, FPdc around next st, ch 1, sk next ch-1 sp, 2 dc in top of beg ch-3. (7 shells)

Row 8: Ch 3, turn, dc in first st, ch 1, sk next ch-1 sp, BPdc around next st, dc in same st, ch 1, sk next ch-1 sp, shell in next ch-2 sp, [ch 1, sk next ch-1 sp, BPdc around next st, ch 1, sk next ch-1 sp, shell in next ch-2 sp], rep between [ ] to 2 ch-1 sps before marked shell, ch 1, sk next ch-1 sp, dc in next st, BPdc around st, ch 1, sk next ch-1 sp, shell in marked sp, ch 1, sk next ch-1 sp, BPdc around next st, dc in same st, ch 1, sk next ch-1 sp, shell in next ch-2 sp; rep between [ ] to last 2 ch-1 sps, ch 1, sk next ch-1 sp, dc in next dc, BPdc around st, ch 1, sk next ch-1 sp, 2 dc in top of beg ch-3.

Row 9: Ch 3, turn, dc in first st, ch 1, sk next ch-1 sp, FPdc around next st, dc in same st, FPdc around next st, ch 1, sk next ch-1 sp, shell in next ch-2 sp, [ch 1, sk next ch-1 sp, FPdc around next st, ch 1, sk next ch-1 sp, shell in next ch-2 sp]; rep between [ ] to 2 ch-1 sps before marked shell, ch 1, sk

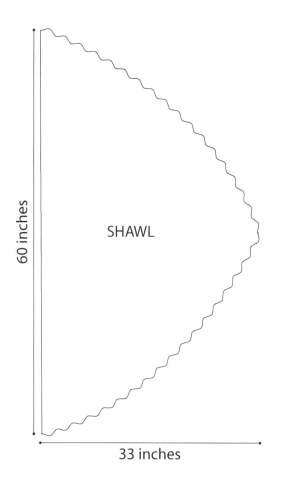

60 inches

SHAWL

33 inches

next ch-1 sp, FPdc around next st, dc in next st, FPdc around st, ch 1, sk next ch-1 sp, shell in marked sp, ch 1, sk next ch-1 sp, FPdc around next st, dc in next st, FPdc around same st, ch 1, sk next ch-1 sp, shell in next ch-2 sp]; rep between [ ] to last 2 ch-1 sps, ch 1, sk next ch-1 sp, FPdc around next st, dc in next st, FPdc around same st, ch 1, sk next ch-1 sp, 2 dc in top of beg ch-3.

Row 10: Ch 3, turn, dc in first st, ch 1, sk next ch-1 sp, BPdc around next st, ch 1, shell in next st, ch 1, BPdc around next st, ch 1, sk next ch-1 sp, shell in next ch-2 sp, [ch 1, sk next ch-1 sp, BPdc around next st, ch 1, sk next ch-1 sp, shell in next ch-2 sp]; rep between [ ] to 2 ch-1 sps before marked shell, ch 1, sk next ch-1 sp, BPdc around next st, ch 1, shell in next st, ch 1, BPdc around next st, ch 1, sk next ch-1 sp, shell in marked sp, ch 1, sk next ch-1 sp, BPdc around next st, ch 1, shell in next st, ch 1, BPdc around next st, ch 1, sk next ch-1 sp, shell in next ch-2 sp; rep between [ ] to last 2 ch-1 sps, ch 1, sk next ch-1 sp, BPdc around next st, ch 1, shell in next st, ch 1, BPdc around next st, ch 1, sk next ch-1 sp, 2 dc in top of beg ch-3. (11 shells)

Row 11: Ch 3, turn, dc in first st, ch 1, sk next ch-1 sp, FPdc around next st, dc in same st, ch 1, sk next ch-1 sp, shell in next ch-2 sp, [ch 1, sk next ch-1 sp, FPdc around next st, ch 1, sk next ch-1 sp, shell in next ch-2 sp], rep between [ ] to 2 ch-1 sps before marked shell, ch 1, sk next ch-1 sp, dc in next st, FPdc around same st, ch 1, sk next ch-1 sp, shell in marked sp, ch 1, sk next ch-1 sp, FPdc around next st, dc in same st, ch 1, sk next ch-1 sp, shell in next ch-2 sp; rep between [ ] to last 2 ch-1 sps, ch 1, sk next ch-1 sp, dc in next st, FPdc around same st, ch 1, sk next ch-1 sp, 2 dc in top of beg ch-3.

Row 12: Ch 3, turn, dc in first st, ch 1. sk next ch-1 sp, BPdc around next st, dc in same st, BPdc around next st, ch 1, shell in next ch-2 sp, [ch 1, sk next ch-1 sp, BPdc around next st, ch 1, sk next ch-1 sp, shell in next ch-2 sp]; rep between [ ] to 2 ch-1 sps before marked shell, ch 1, sk next ch-1 sp, BPdc around next st, dc in next sc, BPdc around same st, ch 1, sk next ch-1 sp, shell in marked sp, ch 1, sk next ch-1 sp, BPdc around next st, dc in same st, BPdc around next st, ch 1, sk next ch-1 sp, shell in next ch-2 sp, ch 1, sk next ch-1 sp; rep between [ ] to last 2 ch-1 sps, ch 1, sk next ch-1 sp, BPdc around next st, dc in next sc, BPdc around same st, ch 1, sk next ch-1 sp, 2 dc in beg ch-3.

Row 13: Ch 3, turn, dc in first st, ch 1, sk next ch-1 sp, FPdc around next st, ch 1, shell in next st, ch 1, FPdc around next st, ch 1, sk next ch-1 sp, shell in next ch-2 sp, [ch 1, sk next ch-1 sp, FPdc around next st, ch 1, sk next ch-1 sp, shell in next ch-2 sp]; rep between [ ] to 2 ch-1 sps before marked shell, ch 1, sk next ch-1 sp, FPdc around next st, ch 1, shell in next st, ch 1, FPdc around next st, ch 1, sk next ch-1 sp, shell in marked sp, ch 1, sk next ch-1 sp, FPdc around next st, ch 1, shell in next st, ch 1, FPdc around next st, ch 1, sk next ch-1 sp, shell in next ch-2 sp; rep between [ ] to last 2 ch-1 sps, FPdc around next st, ch 1, shell in next st, ch 1, FPdc around next st, ch 1, 2 dc in top of beg ch-3. (15 shells)

Rows 14–55: Rep rows 8–13 seven times. (71 shells)

Fasten off.

Finishing

Weave in all ends, block to size.

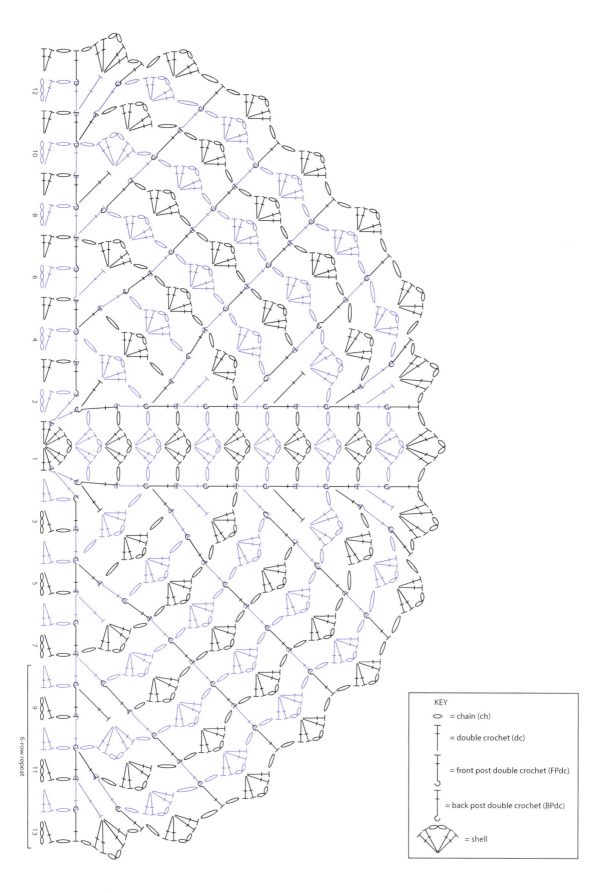

KEY

⬭ = chain (ch)

▮ = double crochet (dc)

▯ = front post double crochet (FPdc)

▯ = back post double crochet (BPdc)

△ = shell

12
10
8
6
4
2
1
3
5
7
9
11
13

6-row repeat

Briar

No matter how hard we try, a garden cannot be truly tamed. Briar is no different. Along the edge of the straight and even rows of this rectangular shawls is a winding vine of pineapple stitches. But don't be fooled by the name – Briar is elegant and soft in a gorgeous lace-weight yarn.

Skill Level

Easy

Finished Size

60 inches (152 cm) long and 15 inches (38 cm) deep

Materials

1200 yards (1097 m) 2-ply laceweight yarn

Model uses Bare Naked Wools Chebris Lace (60% fine wool / 40% yearling mohair; 700 yds / 640 m = 4 oz / 113 g) in the colorway Créme

Size 3.0 mm crochet hook or size needed for gauge

Yarn needle

Gauge

36 dc and 13.5 rows = 4 inches (10 cm) when blocked

Special Stitches

Shell: (2 dc, ch 2, 2 dc) in st or space indicated

Cluster: Yarn over, insert hook in indicated stitch or space and draw up a loop, yarn over and draw through 2 loops on hook

(2 loops remain on hook); yarn over, insert hook in same stitch or space and draw up a loop, yarn over and draw through 2 loops on hook; yarn over and draw through all 3 loops on hook.

dc2tog: Double crochet 2 together—[Yarn over, insert hook in next st and draw up a loop, yarn over and draw through 2 loops on hook] twice, yarn over and draw through all 3 loops on hook.

Pattern Notes

Ch 2 at the end of every row is the turning ch, but does not count as a stitch.

Directions

Ch 119.

Row 1: 2 dc in 3rd ch from hook, ch 1, sk next ch, dc in next ch and in next 88 ch, ch 2, sk 3 ch, shell in next ch, ch 2, sk 3 ch, dc in next ch, ch 2, sk 3 ch, shell in next ch, ch 2, sk 3 ch, (cluster in next ch, ch 2, sk 2 ch) twice, cluster in next ch, ch 2, sk 3 ch, shell in last ch; ch 2, turn.

Row 2: Shell in ch-2 sp of next shell, ch 2, (sk next cluster, cluster in next ch-2 sp, ch 2) twice, sk next cluster and ch-2 sp, shell in ch-2 sp of next shell, ch 2, sk next ch-2 sp, 3 dc in next dc, ch 2, shell in ch-2 sp of next shell, ch 2, sk next ch-2 sp, dc in next dc, *ch 1, sk next dc, dc in next dc; rep from * across to last ch-1 sp, ch 1, sk last ch-1 sp, 2 dc in last dc; ch 2, turn.

Row 3: 2 dc in first dc, sk next ch-1 sp, dc in next dc, *ch 1, sk next ch-1 sp, dc in next dc; rep from * to next ch-2 sp; ch 2, shell in ch-2 sp of next shell, ch 2, sk next ch-2 sp, 2 dc in next dc, dc in next dc, 2 dc in next dc, ch 2, shell in ch-2 sp of next shell, ch 2, sk next cluster, cluster in next ch-2 sp, ch 2, shell in ch-2 sp of next shell; ch 2, turn.

Row 4: Shell in ch-2 sp of next shell, ch 3, sc in top of next cluster, ch 3, shell in ch-2 sp of next shell, ch 2, sk next ch-2 sp, dc in next dc, (ch 1, dc in next dc) 4 times, ch 2, shell in ch-2 sp of next shell, ch 2, sk next ch-2 sp, dc in next dc, *dc in next ch-1-sp, dc in next dc; rep from * to last ch-1 sp, ch 1, sk last ch-1 sp, 2 dc in last dc; ch 2, turn.

Row 5: 2 dc in first dc, ch 1, sk next ch-1 sp, dc in next dc, *ch 1, sk 1 dc, dc in next dc, rep from * to next ch-2 sp, ch 2, shell in ch-2 sp of next shell, ch 2, sk next ch-2 sp, (cluster in next ch-1 sp, ch 2) 4 times, shell in ch-2 sp of next shell, ch 3, shell in ch-2 sp of next shell; ch 2, turn.

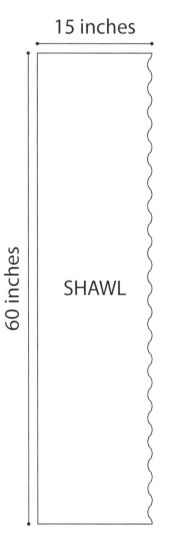

15 inches

60 inches

SHAWL

Row 6: Shell in ch-2 sp of next shell, ch 2, dc in middle ch of next ch-3, ch 2, shell in ch-2 sp of next shell, ch 2, sk next cluster, (cluster in next ch-2 sp, ch 2) 3 times, shell in ch-2 sp of next shell, ch 2, sk next ch-2 sp, dc in next dc, *dc in next ch-1 sp, dc in next dc; rep from * to last ch-1 sp, ch 1, sk last ch-1 sp, 2 dc last dc; ch 2, turn.

Row 7: 2 dc in first dc, ch 1, sk next ch-1 sp, dc in next dc; *ch 1, sk 1 dc, dc in next dc; rep from * to next ch-2 sp, ch 2, shell in ch-2 sp of next shell, ch 2, sk next cluster, (cluster in next ch-2 sp, ch 2) 2 times, shell in ch-2 sp of next shell, ch 2, sk next ch-2 sp, 3 dc in next dc, ch 2, shell in ch-2 sp of next shell; ch 2, turn.

Row 8: Shell in ch-2 sp of next shell, ch 2, sk next ch-2 sp, 2 dc in next dc, dc in next dc, 2 dc in next dc, ch 2, shell in ch-2 sp of next shell, ch 2, sk next cluster, cluster in next ch-2 sp, ch 2, shell in ch-2 sp of next shell, ch 2, sk next ch-2 sp, dc in next dc, *ch 1, dc in next dc; rep from * to last ch-1 sp, ch 1, sk last ch-1 sp, 2 dc in last dc; ch 2, turn.

Row 9: 2 dc in first dc, ch 1, sk next ch-1 sp, dc in next dc; *dc in next ch-1 sp, dc in next dc; rep from * to next ch-2 sp, ch 2, shell in ch-2 sp of next shell, ch 3, sc in top of next cluster, ch 3, shell in ch-2 sp of next shell, ch 2, sk next ch-2 sp, dc in next dc, (ch 1, dc in next dc)

4 times, ch 2, shell in ch-2 sp of next shell; ch 2, turn.

Row 10: Shell in ch-2 sp of next shell, ch 2, sk next ch-2 sp, (cluster in next ch-1 sp, ch 2) 4 times, shell in ch-2 sp of next shell, ch 3, shell in ch-2 sp of next shell, ch 2, sk next ch-2 sp, dc in next dc, *ch 1, sk 1 dc, dc in next dc; rep from * to last ch-1 sp, ch 1, sk last ch-1 sp, 2 dc in last dc; ch 2, turn.

Row 11: 2 dc in first dc, ch 1, sk next ch-1 sp, dc in next dc; *dc in next ch-1 sp, dc in next dc; rep from * to next ch-2 sp, ch 2, sk next ch-2 sp, shell in ch-2 sp of next shell, ch 2, dc in middle ch of next ch-3, ch 2, shell in ch-2 sp of next shell, ch 2, sk next cluster, (cluster in next ch-2 sp, ch 2) 3 times, shell in ch-2 sp of next shell; ch 2, turn.

Rows 12–200: Rep rows 2–11 eighteen times then rows 2–10 once more.

Last Row: 2 dc in first dc, ch 1, sk next ch-1 sp, dc in next dc; *dc in next ch-1 sp, dc in next dc; rep from * to next ch-2 sp,, ch 2, sl st in ch-2 sp of next shell, ch 2, dc in middle ch of next ch-3, ch 2, sl st in ch-2 sp of next shell, ch 2, (sk next cluster, sl st in next ch-2 sp, ch 2) 3 times, sl st in ch-2 sp of next shell; fasten off.

Finishing

Weave in all ends. Block to size.

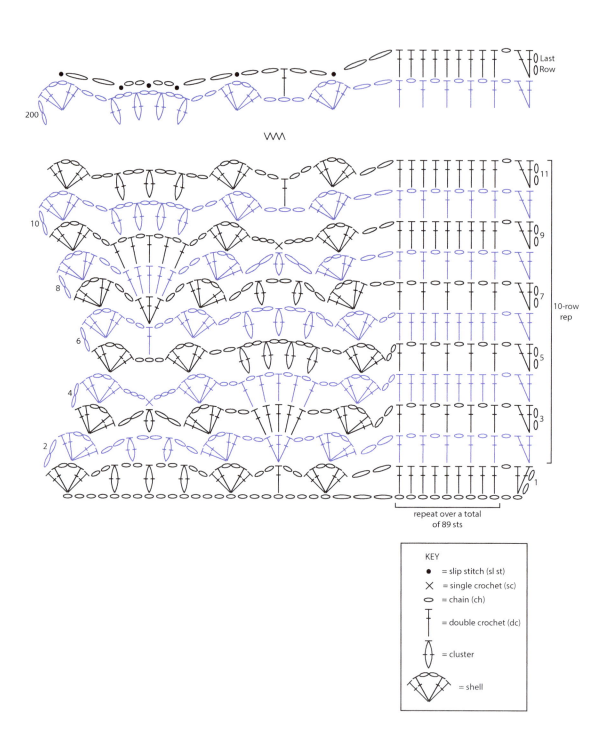

Violaceous

Violaceous represents its meaning of faithfulness and love. Worked in once piece from side to side, it is truly a representation of love for the wearer. Light and airy in a gorgeous purple the person who wears it cannot help but feel all of the love you have put into it.

Skill Level

Intermediate

Finished Size

67 inches (170 cm) wingspan and 15 inches (38 cm) at deepest point

Materials

725 yards (663 m) laceweight yarn

Model uses Happy Fuzzy Yarn Merino Silk Lace (80% merino / 20% tussah silk; 4 oz / 114g = 1000 yds / 915 m) in the colorway Iris

Size 3.0 mm crochet hook or size needed for gauge

Yarn needle

Gauge

22 dc and 11 dc rows = 4 inches (10 cm) when blocked

Special Stitches

Beginning Shell (beg shell): Sl st in each dc to first ch-2 sp, sl st in ch-2 sp, ch 3 (counts as first dc), (2 dc, ch 2, 3 dc) in same sp as last sl st.

Shell: (3 dc, ch 2, 3 dc) in space indicated.

Pattern Notes

Ch 2 at the beginning of every odd row does not count as a stitch. You will always dc in the very first stitch instead of skipping.

Directions

Ch 36.

Increase Section

Row 1: Dc in 3rd ch from hook and in next 21 ch, ch 1, sk 2 ch, 3 dc in next ch, ch 2, 3 dc in next ch, ch 3, sk 2 ch, dc in next ch, 2 dc in next ch, ch 3, sk next 2 ch, 3 dc in next ch, ch 2, 3 dc in last ch. (22 dc in body of shawl; 2 shells and 3 dc in lace edging).

Row 2: Turn, work beg shell, ch 3, sk next ch-3 sp, 2 dc in next dc, dc in next dc, 2 dc in next dc, ch 3, sk next ch-3 sp, shell in next ch-2 sp, ch 1, sk next ch-1 sp, dc in next 12 dc, ch 2, sk 2 dc, dc in each dc to end. (20 dc and 1 ch-2 sp in body; 2 shells and 5 dc in lace edging)

Row 3: Ch 2, turn, dc in each dc to 3 dc before first ch-2 sp, ch 2, sk 2 dc, dc in next dc, 2 dc in next ch-2 sp, dc in next dc, ch 2, sk 2 dc, dc in each dc to last 2 dc before next ch-1 sp, 2 dc in next dc, dc in next dc, ch 1, shell in ch-2 sp of next shell, ch 2, sk next ch-3 sp, 2 dc in next dc, dc in next 3 dc, 2 dc in next dc, ch 2, shell in ch-2 sp of next shell. (19 dc and 2 ch-2 sps in body; 2 shells and 7 dc in lace edging)

Row 4: Turn, work beg shell, ch 2, sk next ch-2 sp, 2 dc in next dc, dc in next 5 dc, 2 dc in next dc, ch 2, shell in ch-2 sp of next shell, ch 1, sk next ch-1 sp, dc in each dc to next ch-2 sp, 2 dc in ch-2 sp, dc in next dc, ch 2, sk 2 dc, dc in next dc, 2 dc in next ch-2 sp, dc in each dc in each dc to end. (21 dc and 1 ch-2 sp in body; 2 shells and 9 dc in lace edging)

Row 5: Ch 2, turn, dc in each dc and 2 dc in each ch-2 sp to last 2 dc before next ch-1 sp, 2

dc in next dc, dc in next dc, ch 1, shell in ch-2 sp of next shell, ch 5, sk next ch-2 sp and next 3 dc, sc in next dc, ch 5, sk next 3 dc, 3 dc in next dc, ch 2, 3 dc in next dc; leave remaining sts unworked. (24 dc in body; 2 shells and 1 sc in lace edging)

Row 6: Turn, work beg shell, ch 3, dc in next 2 ch-5 sps, ch 3, work shell in ch-2 sp of next shell, ch 1, sk next ch-1 sp, dc in each dc in each dc to end. (24

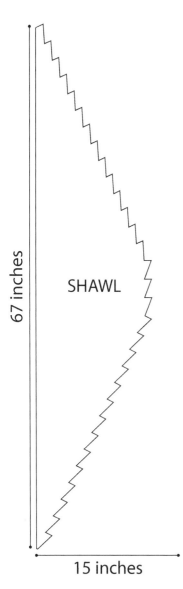

67 inches

SHAWL

15 inches

dc in body; 2 shells and 2 dc in lace edging)

Row 7: Ch 2, turn, dc in each dc to last 2 dc before next ch-1 sp, 2 dc in next dc, dc in next dc, ch 1, shell in ch-2 sp of next shell, ch 3, sk next ch-3 sp, dc in next dc, 2 dc in next dc, ch 3, shell in next ch-2 sp of next shell. (25 dc in body; 2 shells and 3 dc in lace edging)

Row 8: Turn, work beg shell, ch 3, sk next ch-3 sp, 2 dc in next dc, dc in next dc, 2 dc in next dc, ch 3, sk next ch-3 sp, shell in ch-2 sp of next shell, ch 1, sk next ch-1 sp, dc in next 6 dc, ch 2, sk 2 dc, dc in each dc to end.

Rows 9–13: Rep rows 3–7. (28 dc in body; 2 shells and 3 dc in lace edging)

Row 14: Turn, work beg shell, ch 3, sk next 3 dc, 2 dc in next dc, dc in next dc, 2 dc in next dc, ch 3, sk next 3 dc, work shell in next ch-2 sp, ch 1, sk next ch-1 sp, dc in next 18 dc, ch 2, sk 2 dc, dc in each dc to end.

Rows 15–19: Rep rows 3–7. (31 dc in body)

Rows 20–25: Rep rows 2–7. (34 dc in body)

Row 26: Turn, work beg shell, ch 3, sk next 3 dc, 2 dc in next dc, dc in next dc, 2 dc in next dc, ch 3, sk next 3 dc, work shell in next ch-2 sp, ch 1, sk next ch-1 sp, dc in next 6 dc, *ch 2, sk 2 dc, dc in next 16 dc;

rep from * until there are fewer than 28 dc remaining, ch 2, sk 2 dc, dc in each dc to end.

Row 27: Ch 2, turn, *dc in each dc to next ch-2 sp, ch 2, sk 2 dc, dc in next dc, 2 dc in next ch-2 sp, dc in next dc, ch 2, sk 2 dc; rep from * until all ch-2 sps in body have been worked over, dc in each dc to last 2 dc before next ch-1 sp, 2 dc in next dc, dc in next dc, ch 1, shell in ch-2 sp of next shell, ch 2, sk 3 dc, 2 dc in next dc, dc in next 3 dc, 2 dc in next dc, ch 2, shell in ch-2 sp of next shell.

Row 28: Turn, work beg shell, ch 2, sk next 3 dc, 2 dc in next dc, dc in next 5 dc, 2 dc in next dc, ch 2, shell in ch-2 sp of next shell, ch 1, sk next ch-1 sp, * dc in each dc to next ch-2 sp, 2 dc in ch-2 sp, dc in next dc, ch 2, sk 2 dc, dc in next dc, 2 dc in next ch-2 sp, rep from * until all ch-2 sps have been worked into, dc in each dc in each dc to end.

Rows 29–31: Rep rows 5–7. (37 dc in body)

Row 32: Turn, work beg shell, ch 3, sk next 3 dc, 2 dc in next dc, dc in next dc, 2 dc in next dc, ch 3, sk next 3 dc, work shell in next ch-2 sp, ch 1, sk next ch-1 sp, dc in next 2 dc, *dc in next 16 dc, ch 2, sk 2 dc; rep from * until fewer than 23 dc remain, dc in each dc to end.

Rows 33–37: Rep rows 27–31. (40 dc in body)

Row 38: Turn, work beg shell, ch 3, sk next 3 dc, 2 dc in next dc, dc in next dc, 2 dc in next dc, ch 3, sk next 3 dc, work shell in next ch-2 sp, ch 1, sk next ch-1 sp, dc in next 12 dc, *ch 2, sk 2 dc, dc in next 16 dc; rep from * until fewer than 28 dc remain, ch 2, sk 2 dc, dc in each dc to end.

Rows 39–43: Rep rows 27–31. (43 dc in body)

Rows 44–61: Rep rows 26–43. (52 dc in body)

Rows 62–79: Rep rows 26–43. (61 dc in body)

Rows 80–82: Rep rows 26–28. (62 dc in body)

Center Section

Row 83: Ch 2, turn, dc in each dc to next ch-1 sp, ch 1, shell in ch-2 sp of next shell, ch 5, sk next ch-2 sp and next 3 dc, sc in next dc, ch 5, sk next 3 dc, 3 dc in next dc, ch 2, 3 dc in next dc; leave remaining sts unworked.

Row 84: Turn, work beg shell, ch 3, dc in next 2 ch-5 sps, ch 3, work shell in ch-2 sp of next shell, ch 1, sk next ch-1 sp, dc in each dc in each dc to end.

Row 85: Ch 2, turn, dc in each dc to next ch-1 sp, ch 1, shell in ch-2 sp of next shell, ch 3, sk next ch-3 sp, dc in next dc, 2 dc in next dc, ch 3, shell in next ch-2 sp of next shell.

Row 86: Turn, work beg shell, ch 3, sk next 3 dc, 2 dc in next dc, dc in next dc, 2 dc in next dc, ch 3, sk next 3 dc, work shell in next ch-2 sp, ch 1, sk next ch-1 sp, [dc in next 16 dc, ch 2, sk 2 dc] 3 times, dc in each dc to end.

Row 87: Ch 2, turn, *dc in each dc to next ch-2 sp, ch 2, sk 2 dc, dc in next dc, 2 dc in next ch-2 sp, dc in next dc, ch 2, sk 2 dc; rep from * until all ch-2 sps in body have been worked over, dc in each dc to ch-1 sp, ch 1, shell in ch-2 sp of next shell, ch 2, sk 3 dc, 2 dc in next dc, dc in next 3 dc, 2 dc in next dc, ch 2, shell in ch-2 sp of next shell.

Row 88: Turn, work beg shell, ch 2, sk next 3 dc, 2 dc in next dc, dc in next 5 dc, 2 dc in next dc, ch 2, shell in ch-2 sp of next shell, ch 1, sk next ch-1 sp, * dc in each dc to next ch-2 sp, 2 dc in ch-2 sp, dc in next dc, ch 2, sk 2 dc, dc in next dc, 2 dc in next ch-2 sp, rep from * until all ch-2 sps have been worked into, dc in each dc in each dc to end.

Rows 89–91: Rep rows 83–85.

Row 92: Turn, work beg shell, ch 3, sk next 3 dc, 2 dc in next dc, dc in next dc, 2 dc in next dc, ch 3, sk next 3 dc, work shell in next ch-2 sp, ch 1, sk next ch-1 sp, dc in next 7 dc, ch 2, sk 2 dc, [dc in next 16 dc, ch 2, sk 2 dc] twice, dc in each dc to end.

Rows 93–97: Rep Rows 87–91.

Rows 98–103: Rep rows 86–91.

Decrease Section

Row 104: Rep Row 92.

Row 105: Ch 2, turn, *dc in each dc to next ch-2 sp, ch 2, sk 2 dc, dc in next dc, 2 dc in next ch-2 sp, dc in next dc, ch 2, sk 2 dc; rep from * until all ch-2 sps in body have been worked over, dc in each dc to 3 dc before ch-1 sp, dc2tog, dc in next dc, ch 1, shell in ch-2 sp of next shell, ch 2, sk 3 dc, 2 dc in next dc, dc in next 3 dc, 2 dc in next dc, ch 2, shell in ch-2 sp of next shell.

Row 106: Turn, work beg shell, ch 2, sk next 3 dc, 2 dc in next dc, dc in next 5 dc, 2 dc in next dc, ch 2, shell in ch-2 sp of next shell, ch 1, sk next ch-1 sp, * dc in each dc to next ch-2 sp, 2 dc in ch-2 sp, dc in next dc, ch 2, sk 2 dc, dc in next dc, 2 dc in next ch-2 sp, rep from * until all ch-2 sps have been worked into, dc in each dc in each dc to end.

Row 107: Ch 2, turn, dc in each dc to last 3 dc before next ch-1 sp, dc2tog, dc in next dc, ch 1, shell in ch-2 sp of next shell, ch 5, sk next ch-2 sp and

next 3 dc, sc in next dc, ch 5, sk next 3 dc, 3 dc in next dc, ch 2, 3 dc in next dc; leave remaining sts unworked.

Row 108: Turn, work beg shell, ch 3, dc in next 2 ch-5 sps, ch 3, work shell in ch-2 sp of next shell, ch 1, sk next ch-1 sp, dc in each dc in each dc to end.

Row 109: Ch 2, turn, dc in each dc to last 3 dc before next ch-1 sp, dc2tog, dc in next dc, ch 1, shell in ch-2 sp of next shell, ch 3, sk next ch-3 sp, dc in next dc, 2 dc in next dc, ch 3, shell in next ch-2 sp of next shell. (59 dc in body)

Row 110: Turn, work beg shell, ch 3, sk next 3 dc, 2 dc in next dc, dc in next dc, 2 dc in next dc, ch 3, sk next 3 dc, work shell in next ch-2 sp, ch 1, sk next ch-1 sp, dc in next 13 dc, *ch 2, sk 2 dc, dc in next 16 dc; rep from * until fewer than 28 dc remain, ch 2, sk 2 dc, dc in each dc to end.

Rows 111–115: Rep rows 105–109. (56 dc in body)

Row 116: Turn, work beg shell, ch 3, sk next 3 dc, 2 dc in next dc, dc in next dc, 2 dc in next dc, ch 3, sk next 3 dc, work shell in next ch-2 sp, ch 1, sk next ch-1 sp, dc in next 19 dc, *ch 2, sk 2 dc, dc in next 16 dc; rep from * until fewer than 28 dc reman, ch 2, sk 2 dc, dc in each dc to end.

Rows 117–121: Rep rows 105–109. (53 dc in body)

Row 122: Turn, work beg shell, ch 3, sk next 3 dc, 2 dc in next dc, dc in next dc, 2 dc in next dc, ch 3, sk next 3 dc, work shell in next ch-2 sp, ch 1, sk next ch-1 sp, dc in next 7 dc, *ch 2, sk 2 dc, dc in next 16 dc; rep * from until fewer than 28 dc remain, ch 2, sk 2 dc, dc in each dc to end.

Rows 123–127: Rep rows 105–109 (50 dc in body)

Rows 128–145: Rep rows 110–127. (41 dc in body)

Rows 146–151: Rep rows 110–115. (38 dc in body)

Row 152: Turn, work beg shell, ch 3, sk next 3 dc, 2 dc in next dc, dc in next dc, 2 dc in next dc, ch 3, sk next 3 dc, work shell in next ch-2 sp, ch 1, sk next ch-1 sp, dc in next 19 dc, ch 2, sk 2 dc, dc in each dc to end.

Rows 153–163: Rep rows 117–127. (32 dc in body)

Row 164: Turn, work beg shell, ch 3, sk next 3 dc, 2 dc in next dc, dc in next dc, 2 dc in next dc, ch 3, sk next 3 dc, work shell in next ch-2 sp, ch 1, sk next ch-1 sp, dc in next 13 dc, ch 2, sk 2 dc, dc in each dc to end.

Rows 165–169: Rep rows 105–109. (29 dc in body)

Row 170: Turn, work beg shell, ch 3, sk next 3 dc, 2 dc

in next dc, dc in next dc, 2 dc in next dc, ch 3, sk next 3 dc, work shell in next ch-2 sp, ch 1, sk next ch-1 sp, dc in next 19 dc, ch 2, sk 2 dc; dc in each dc to end.

Rows 171–175: Rep rows 105–109. (26 dc in body)

Row 176: Turn, work beg shell, ch 3, sk next 3 dc, 2 dc in next dc, dc in next dc, 2 dc in next dc, ch 3, sk next 3 dc, work shell in next ch-2 sp, ch 1, sk next ch-1 sp, dc in next 7 dc, ch 2, sk 2 dc, dc in each dc to end.

Rows 177–181: Rep rows 105–109. (23 dc in body)

Row 182: Turn, work beg shell, ch 3, sk next 3 dc, 2 dc in next

dc, dc in next dc, 2 dc in next dc, ch 3, sk next 3 dc, work shell in next ch-2 sp, ch 1, sk next ch-1 sp, dc in next 13 dc, ch 2, sk 2 dc; dc in each dc to end.

Rows 183 and 184: Rep rows 105 and 106.

Row 185: Ch 2, turn, dc in next 8 dc, 2 dc in next ch-2 sp, dc in each dc to next ch-1 sp, ch 1, sl st in next ch-2 sp, ch 5, sk next ch-2 sp and next 3 dc, sc in next dc, ch 7, sk next 8 dc, sl st in next ch-2 sp; leave remaining sts unworked. Fasten off.

Finishing

Weave in all ends. Block to size.

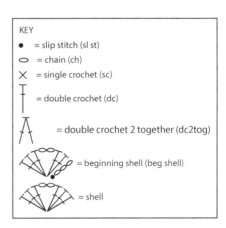

KEY

● = slip stitch (sl st)

⌒ = chain (ch)

✕ = single crochet (sc)

╤ = double crochet (dc)

⋀ = double crochet 2 together (dc2tog)

= beginning shell (beg shell)

= shell

Increase Section

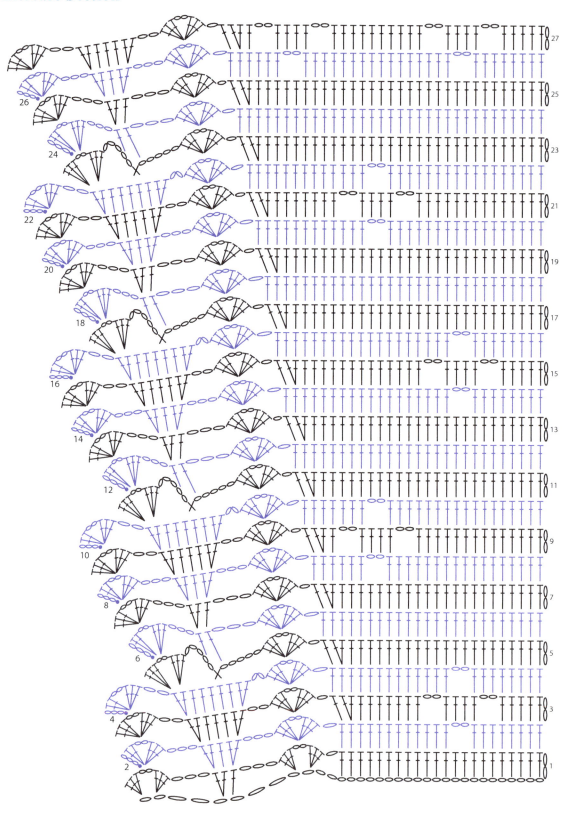

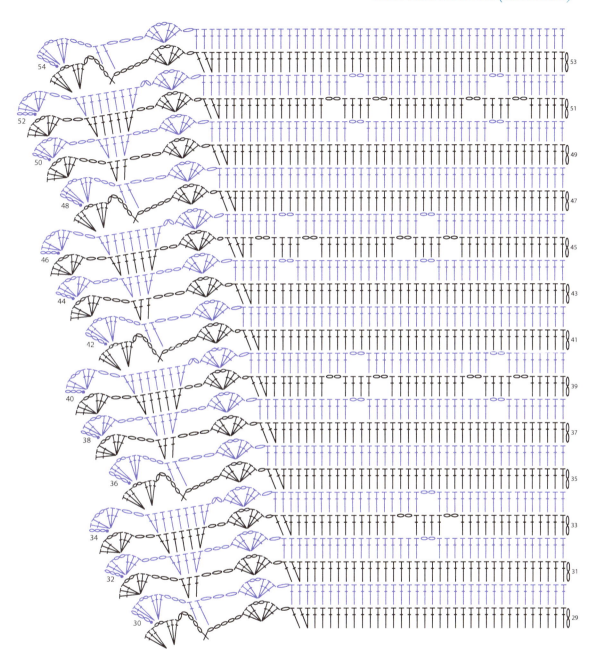

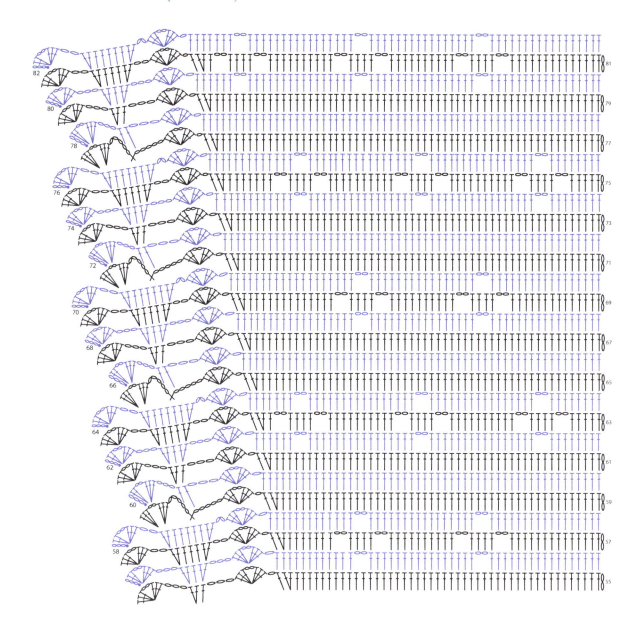

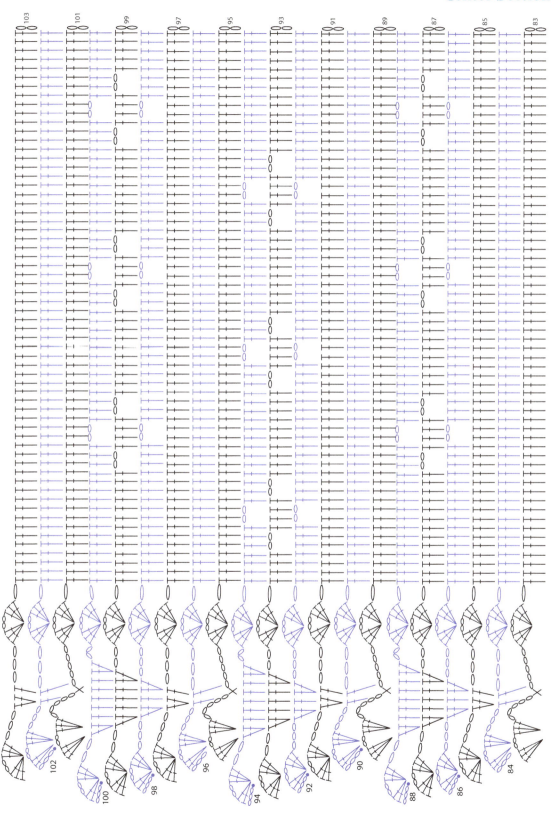

Decrease Section

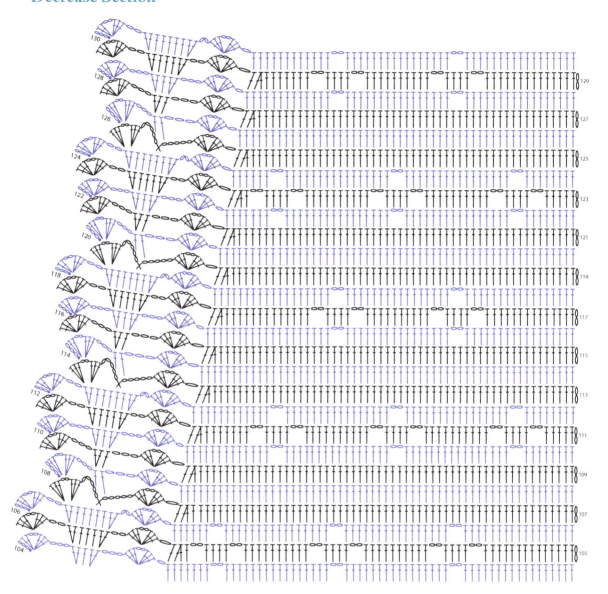

A Garden of Shawls

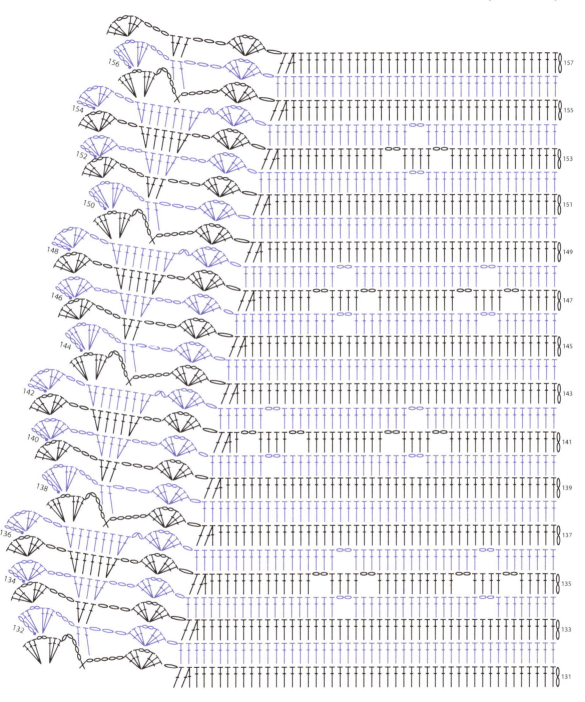

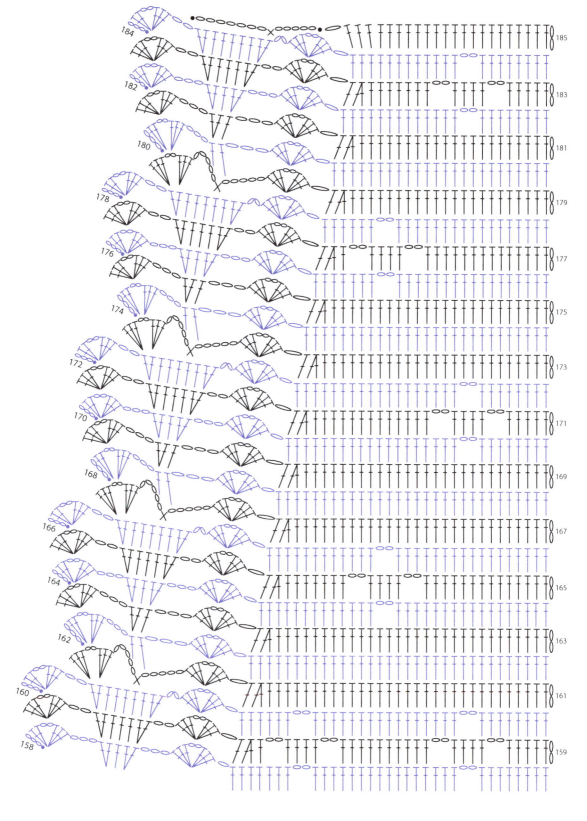

Foliole

Foliole represents the new life of a beautiful spring. Beguiling us with interlacing fronds with a lacy leaf edge, your wardrobe will have a touch of your garden any time of the year.

Skill Level

Intermediate

Finished Size

75 inches (190.5 cm) long by 19 inches (48 cm) wide blocked

Materials

960 yards (878 m) fingering weight yarn

Model uses The Fiber Seed Sprout (90% superwash merino / 10% nylon; 5 oz / 140g = 480 yds / 439 m) in the colorway #S038 Sour Apple

US size D/3 (3.25mm) crochet hook or size needed for gauge

Yarn needle

Gauge

In pattern (blocked)
1 repeat = 3 inches (7.62 cm)
6.5 rows = 4 inches (10 cm)

Special Stitches

dc4tog: Double crochet 4 together – [Yarn over, insert hook in next stitch and draw up a loop, yarn over and draw through 2 loops on hook] 4 times; yarn over and draw through all 5 loops on hook.

Directions

Ch 87.

Row 1: Dc in 8th ch from the hook, ch 3, sk 3 ch, [dc in next 3 ch, ch 2, sk 2 ch] twice, *dc in next 5 ch, ch 2, sk 2 ch; rep from * 8 times, dc in last 3 ch.

Row 2: Ch 7 (counts as first dc and ch-4 sp), turn, sk first ch-2 sp, [2 dc in next dc, dc in next dc, ch 1, sk 1 dc, dc in next dc, 2 dc in next dc, ch 4, dc in center dc of next 5-dc group, ch 4, sk next 2 dc] 4 times, 2 dc in next dc, dc in next dc, ch 1, sk next dc, dc in next dc, 2 dc in next dc, ch 4, dc in last dc of next 3-dc group, ch 2, dc in next 3 dc, ch 3, dc in next dc, 4 dc in last sp.

Row 3: Ch 7, turn, 2 dc in first dc, dc in next dc, ch 1, sk next dc, dc in next dc, 2 dc in next dc, ch 3, dc in next 3 dc, ch 2, dc in next dc, [ch 4, dc in next 3 dc, ch 1, dc in next 3 dc, ch 4, dc in next dc] 5 times working the last dc in 3rd ch of beg ch-7.

Row 4: Ch 7, turn, sk next ch-4 sp, dc in next 3 dc, ch 1, dc in next 3 dc, [ch 4, dc in next dc, ch 4, dc in next 3 dc, ch 1, dc in next 3 dc] 4 times, ch 4, dc in next dc, ch 2, dc in next 3 dc, ch 3, 2 dc in next dc, dc in next 2 dc, ch 1, dc in next 2 dc, 2 dc in next dc; leave beg ch unworked.

Row 5: Ch 7, turn, dc in first 4 dc, sk next ch-1 sp, dc in next 4 dc, ch 3, dc in next 3 dc, ch 2, dc in next dc, 2 dc in next ch-4 sp, ch 3, dc2tog over next 2 dc, dc in next dc, dc in next ch-1 sp, dc in next dc, dc2tog, [ch 3, 2 dc in next ch-4 sp, dc in next dc, 2 dc in next ch-4 sp, ch 3, dc2tog over next 2 dc, dc in next dc, dc in next ch-1 sp, dc in next dc, dc2tog] 4 times, ch 3, 2 dc in beg ch-sp, dc in 3rd ch of beg ch-7.

Row 6: Ch 3, turn, dc in next dc, 2 dc in next dc, ch 4, sk 2 dc, dc in next dc, ch 4, sk next ch-3 sp, [2 dc in next dc, dc in next dc, ch 1, sk 1 dc, dc in next dc, 2 dc in next dc, ch 4, sk next 2 dc, dc in next dc, ch 4, sk next 2 dc] 3 times, 2 dc in next dc, dc in next dc, ch 1, sk 1 dc, dc in next dc, 2 dc in next dc, ch 4, sk next 2 dc, dc in next dc, ch 4, sk next ch-3 sp, 2 dc in next dc, dc in next 2 dc, ch 2, dc in next 2 dc, (dc, ch 3, dc) in next dc, ch 3, [dc2tog] 4 times; leave beg ch unworked.

Row 7: Ch 7, turn, dc4tog, ch 3, (dc, ch 3, dc) in next dc, ch 3, dc in next 3 dc, ch 2, dc in next 4 dc, ch 4, dc in next dc, [ch 4, dc in next 3 dc, ch 1, dc in next 3 dc, ch 4, dc in next dc] 4 times, ch 4, dc in next 3 dc, dc in top of beg ch-3.

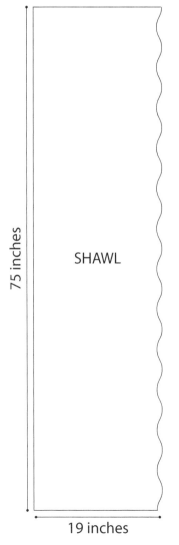

75 inches

SHAWL

19 inches

Row 8: Ch 3, turn, dc in next 3 dc, ch 4, dc in next dc, [ch 4, dc in next 3 dc, ch 1, dc in next 3 dc, ch 4, dc in next dc] 4 times, ch 4, dc in next 4 dc, ch 2, dc in next 3 dc, ch 3, dc in next dc, 3 dc in next ch-3 sp, dc in next dc, leave remaining sts unworked.

Row 9: Ch 7, turn, 2 dc in first dc, dc in next dc, ch 1, sk next dc, dc in next dc, 2 dc in next dc, ch 3, dc in next 3 dc, ch 2, dc in next 2 dc, dc2tog, ch 3, 2 dc in next ch-4 sp, dc in next dc, 2 dc in next ch-4 sp, [ch 3, dc2tog over next 2 dc, dc in next dc, dc in ch-1 sp, dc in next dc, dc2tog, ch 3, 2 dc in next ch-4 sp, dc in next dc, 2 dc in next ch-4 sp] 4 times, ch 3, dc2tog, dc in next dc, dc in top of beg ch-3.

Row 10: Ch 7 (counts as first dc and ch-4 sp), turn, sk next ch-3 sp, [2 dc in next dc, dc in next dc, ch 1, sk 1 dc, dc in next dc, 2 dc in next dc, ch 4, sk next 2 dc, dc in next dc, ch 4, sk next 2 dc] 4 times, 2 dc in next dc, dc in next dc, ch 1, sk 1 dc, dc in next dc, 2 dc in next dc, ch 4, sk next 2 dc, dc in next dc, ch 2, dc in next 3 dc, ch 3, 2 dc in next dc, dc in next 2 dc, ch 1, sk next ch-1 sp, dc in next 2 dc, 2 dc in next dc; leave beg ch unworked.

Row 11: Ch 7, turn, dc in first 4 dc, sk next ch-1 sp, dc in next 4 dc, ch 3, dc in next 3 dc, ch 2, dc in next dc, [ch 4, dc in next 3 dc, ch 1, dc in next 3 dc, ch 4,

dc in next dc] 5 times working the last dc in 3rd ch of beg ch-7.

Row 12: Ch 7, turn, sk next ch-4 sp, dc in next 3 dc, ch 1, dc in next 3 dc, [ch 4, dc in next dc, ch 4, dc in next 3 dc, ch 1, dc in next 3 dc] 4 times, ch 4, dc in next dc, ch 2, dc in next 2 dc, (dc, ch 3, dc) in next dc, ch 3, [dc2tog] 4 times; leave beg ch unworked.

Row 13: Ch 7, turn, dc4tog, ch 3, (dc, ch 3, dc) in next dc, ch 3, dc in next 3 dc, ch 2, dc in next dc, 2 dc in next ch-4 sp, ch 3, dc2tog over next 2 dc, dc in next dc, dc in next ch-1 sp, dc in next dc, dc2tog, [ch 3, 2 dc in next ch-4 sp, dc in next dc, 2 dc in next ch-4 sp, ch 3, dc2tog over next 2 dc, dc in next dc, dc in next ch-1 sp, dc in next dc, dc2tog] 4 times, ch 3, 2 dc in beg ch-sp, dc in 3rd ch of beg ch-7.

Row 14: Ch 3, turn, dc in next dc, 2 dc in next dc, ch 4, sk 2 dc, dc in next dc, ch 4, sk next ch-3 sp, [2 dc in next dc, dc in next dc, ch 1, sk 1 dc, dc in next dc, 2 dc in next dc, ch 4, sk next 2 dc, dc in next dc, ch 4, sk next 2 dc] 3 times, 2 dc in next dc, dc in next dc, ch 1, sk 1 dc, dc in next dc, 2 dc in next dc, ch 4, sk next 2 dc, dc in next dc, ch 4, sk next ch-3 sp, 2 dc in next dc, dc in next 2 dc, ch 2, dc in next 3 dc, ch 3, dc in next dc, 3 dc in next ch-3 sp, dc in next dc, leave remaining sts unworked.

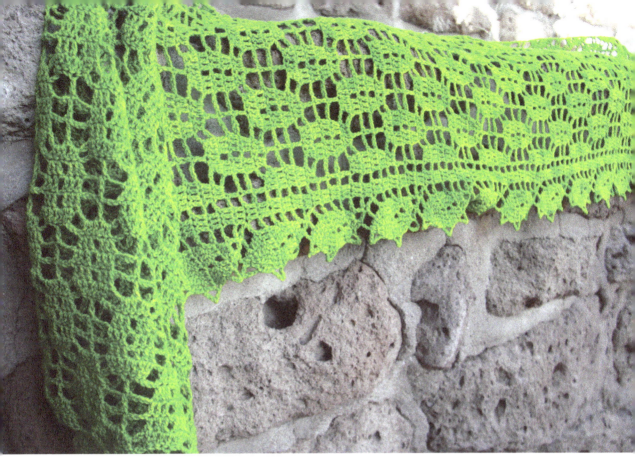

Row 15: Ch 7, turn, 2 dc in first dc, dc in next dc, ch 1, sk next dc, dc in next dc, 2 dc in next dc, ch 3, dc in next 3 dc, ch 2, dc in next 4 dc, ch 4, dc in next dc, [ch 4, dc in next 3 dc, ch 1, dc in next 3 dc, ch 4, dc in next dc] 4 times, ch 4, dc in next 3 dc and in top of beg ch-3.

Row 16 : Ch 3, turn, dc in next 3 dc, ch 4, dc in next dc, [ch 4, dc in next 3 dc, ch 1, dc in next 3 dc, ch 4, dc in next dc] 4 times, ch 4, dc in next 4 dc, ch 2, dc in next 3 dc, ch 3, 2 dc in next dc, dc in next 2 dc, ch 1, dc in next 2 dc, 2 dc in next dc; leave beg ch unworked.

Row 17: Ch 7, turn, dc in first 4 dc, sk next ch-1 sp, dc in next 4 dc, ch 3, dc in next 3 dc, ch 2,

dc in next 2 dc, dc2tog, ch 3, 2 dc in next ch-4 sp, dc in next dc, 2 dc in next ch-4 sp, [ch 3, dc2tog over next 2 dc, dc in next dc, dc in next ch-1 sp, dc in next dc, dc2tog, ch 3, 2 dc in next ch-4 sp, dc in next dc, 2 dc in next ch-4 sp] 4 times, ch 3, dc2tog, dc in next dc, dc in top of beg ch-3.

Row 18: Ch 7 (counts as first dc and ch-4 sp), turn, sk next ch-3 sp, [2 dc in next dc, dc in next dc, ch 1, sk 1 dc, dc in next dc, 2 dc in next dc, ch 4, sk next 2 dc, dc in next dc, ch 4, sk next 2 dc] 4 times, 2 dc in next dc, dc in next dc, ch 1, sk 1 dc, dc in next dc, 2 dc in next dc, ch 4, sk next 2 dc, dc in next dc, ch 2, dc in next 2 dc, (dc, ch 3, dc) in next dc, ch 3,

[dc2tog] 4 times; leave beg ch unworked.

Row 19: Ch 7, turn, dc4tog, ch 3, (dc, ch 3, dc) in next dc, ch 3, dc in next 3 dc, ch 2, dc in next dc, [ch 4, dc in next 3 dc, ch 1, dc in next 3 dc, ch 4, dc in next dc] 5 times working the last dc in 3rd ch of beg ch-7.

Row 20: Ch 7, turn, sk next ch-4 sp, dc in next 3 dc, ch 1, dc in next 3 dc, [ch 4, dc in next dc, ch 4, dc in next 3 dc, ch 1, dc in next 3 dc] 4 times, ch 4, dc in next dc, ch 2, dc in next 3 dc, ch 3, dc in next dc, 3 dc in next ch-3 sp, dc in next dc, leave remaining sts unworked.

Row 21: Ch 7, turn, 2 dc in first dc, dc in next dc, ch 1, sk next dc, dc in next dc, 2 dc in next dc, ch 3, dc in next 3 dc, ch 2, dc in next dc, 2 dc in next ch-4 sp, ch 3, dc2tog over next 2 dc, dc in next dc, dc in next ch-1 sp, dc in next dc, dc2tog, [ch 3, 2 dc in next ch-4 sp, dc in next dc, 2 dc in next ch-4 sp, ch 3, dc2tog over next 2 dc, dc in next dc, dc in ch-1 sp, dc in next dc, dc2tog] 4r times, ch 3, 2 dc in ch-4 sp, dc in 3rd ch of beg ch-7.

Row 22: Ch 3, turn, dc in next dc, 2 dc in next dc, ch 4, sk 2 dc, dc in next dc, ch 4, sk next ch-3 sp, [2 dc in next dc, dc in next dc, ch 1, sk 1 dc, dc in next dc, 2 dc in next dc, ch 4, sk next 2 dc, dc in next dc, ch 4, sk next 2 dc] 3 times, 2 dc in next dc, dc in next dc, ch 1, sk 1 dc, dc in next dc, 2 dc in next dc, ch 4, sk next 2 dc, dc in next dc, ch 4, sk next ch-3 sp, 2 dc in next dc, dc in next 2 dc, ch 2, dc in next 3 dc, ch 3, 2 dc in next dc, dc in next 2 dc, ch 1, dc in next 2 dc, 2 dc in next dc; leave beg ch unworked.

Row 23: Ch 7, turn, dc in first 4 dc, sk next ch-1 sp, dc in next

4 dc, ch 3, dc in next 3 dc, ch 2, dc in next 4 dc, ch 4, dc in next dc, [ch 4, dc in next 3 dc, ch 1, dc in next 3 dc, ch 4, dc in next dc] 4 times, ch 4, dc in next 3 dc, dc in top of beg ch-3.

Row 24: Ch 3, turn, dc in next 3 dc, ch 4, dc in next dc, [ch 4, dc in next 3 dc, ch 1, dc in next 3 dc, ch 4, dc in next dc] 4 times, ch 4, dc in next 4 dc, ch 2, dc in next 2 dc, (dc, ch 3, dc) in next dc, ch 3, (dc2tog) 4 times; leave beg ch unworked.

Row 25: Ch 7, turn, dc4tog, ch 3, (dc, ch 3, dc) in next dc, ch 3, dc in next 3 dc, ch 2, dc in next 2 dc, dc2tog, ch 3, 2 dc in next ch-4 sp, dc in next dc, 2 dc in next ch-4 sp, [ch 3, dc2tog over next 2 dc, dc in next dc, dc in ch-1 sp, dc in next dc, dc2tog, ch 3, 2 dc in next ch-4 sp, dc in next dc, 2 dc in next ch-4 sp] 4 times, ch 3, dc2tog, dc in next dc, dc in top of beg ch-3.

Row 26: Ch 7 (counts as first dc and ch-4 sp), turn, sk next ch-3 sp, [2 dc in next dc, dc in next dc, ch 1, sk 1 dc, dc in

next dc, 2 dc in next dc, ch 4, sk next 2 dc, dc in next dc, ch 4, sk next 2 dc] 4 times, 2 dc in next dc, dc in next dc, ch 1, sk 1 dc, dc in next dc, 2 dc in next dc, ch 4, sk next 2 dc, dc in next dc, ch 2, dc in next 3 dc, ch 3, dc in next dc, 3 dc in next ch-3 sp, dc in next dc; leave remaining sts unworked.

Rep rows 3–26 three times more then rows 3–25 once.

Last Row: Ch 7 (counts as first dc and ch-4 sp), turn, sk next ch-3 sp, [2 dc in next dc, dc in next dc, ch 1, sk 1 dc, dc in next dc, 2 dc in next dc, ch 4, sk next 2 dc, dc in next dc, ch 4, sk next 2 dc] 4 times, 2 dc in next dc, dc in next dc, ch 1, sk 1 dc, dc in next dc, 2 dc in next dc, ch 4, sk next 2 dc, dc in next dc, ch 2, dc in next 3 dc, ch 3, sk next ch 3 sp, sl st in next ch-3 sp.

Fasten off.

Finishing
Weave in all ends. Block to finished measurements.

KEY

●	= slip stitch (sl st)
⬯	= chain (ch)
⊤	= double crochet (dc)

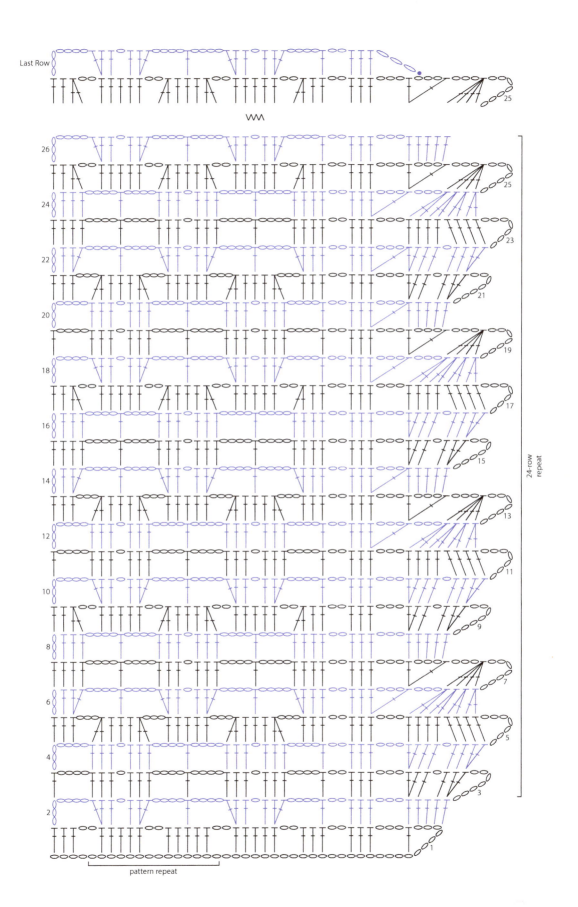

Last Row

VVVVV

26

24

22

20

18

16

14

12

10

8

6

4

2

25

23

21

19

17

15

13

11

9

7

5

3

1

24-row repeat

pattern repeat

Enchantment

Enchantment embodies the simple pleasure we feel when spending time in the garden. Soft yak yarn envelops us with a simple top-down triangular shawl edged with a gorgeous surprise of lace that charms both the maker and the wearer.

Skill Level

Easy

Finished Size

55 inches (140 cm) wide by 27 inches (69 cm) deep (blocked with edging)

Materials

1200 yards (1098 m) fingering weight yarn

Blue Moon Fiber Arts Yaksi Fingering (60% wool / 20% yak / 20% silk; 96 g / 3.38 oz = 356 m / 390 yds) in the colorway "True Blood" Red

US size F/5 (3.75 mm) crochet hook or size needed for gauge

Yarn needle

Gauge

In pattern, 20 dc and 8 rows = 4 inches (10 cm) when blocked

Pattern Notes

Do not skip the first dc when starting a new row unless otherwise indicated.

The ch-4 at the beginning of each row counts as the first dc and ch-1 space.

Directions

Ch 5.

Row 1: Dc in 5th ch from hook – skipped chs count as first dc and ch-1 sp –, (ch 1, dc in same ch) three times more. PM in middle dc for stitch placement. (5 dc and 4 ch-1 sps)

Row 2: Ch 4, turn; dc in first dc, dc in each ch-1 sp and dc to marked stitch; (dc, ch 1, dc, ch 1, dc) in marked stitch, PM in middle dc for stitch placement, dc in each ch-1 sp and dc across to turning ch-sp, dc in turning ch-sp, (dc, ch 1, dc) in 3rd ch or ch-4 turning ch. (13 dc and 4 ch-1 sps)

Row 3: Ch 4, turn; dc in first dc, dc in next ch-1 sp, dc in each dc to next ch-1 sp, dc in next ch-1 sp, (dc, ch 1, dc, ch 1, dc) in marked stitch, PM in middle dc for stitch placement; dc in next ch-1 sp, dc in each dc to turning ch-sp, dc in turning ch-sp, work(dc, ch 1, dc) in 3rd ch of ch-4 turning ch. (21 dc and 4 ch-1 sps)

Row 4: Ch 4, turn; dc in first dc, dc in next ch -1 sp, ch 1, sk next dc *dc in next dc, ch 1, sk next dc; rep from * across to ch-1 sp before marked st; dc in ch-1 sp, (dc, ch 1, dc, ch 1, dc) in marked stich, PM in middle dc for stitch placement; dc in next ch-1 sp, ch 1 sk next dc, +dc in next dc, ch 1, sk next dc; rep from + across to turning ch-sp; dc in turning ch-sp, (dc, ch 1, dc) in 3rd ch of ch-4 turning ch. (19 dc and 14 ch-1 sps)

Rows 5–7: Ch 4, turn; dc in first dc, dc in each dc and ch-1 sp to marked stitch; (dc, ch 1, dc, ch 1, dc) in marked stich, PM in middle dc for stitch placement; dc in each dc and ch-1 sp across to turning ch-sp, dc in turning ch-sp,; (dc, ch 1, dc) in 3rd ch of ch-4 turning ch. (53 dc and 4 ch-1 sps)

Rows 8–34: Repeat rows 4–7 nine times more. (341 dc and 4 ch-1 sps)

Do not fasten off.

Edging

Row 1: Ch 5 (counts as sc, ch 4), turn, sk first dc, sk first ch-1 sp, sc in next dc, (ch 4, sk next 2 dc, sc in next dc) 56 times (last sc should be in the last dc before first ch-1 sp in center of point), ch 4, sk next ch-1 sp, sk marked dc, sk next ch-1 sp, sc in next dc, (ch 4, sk next 2 dc, sc in next dc) 56 times, ch 4, sc in 3rd ch of ch-4 turning ch. (115 ch-4 sps)

Row 2: Ch 3, turn, sc in first ch-4 sp, *ch 2, (dc, ch 2) 4 times in next ch 4 sp, sc in next ch-4 sp; rep from * across.

Row 3: Ch 5 (counts as dc, ch 2), turn, dc in first sc, * sk next ch-2 sp and dc, [sc in next ch-2 sp, ch 3] twice, sc in next ch-2 sp **, i(dc, [ch 3, dc] twice) in next sc, rep from * across, ending at ** on last rep, (dc, ch 2, dc) in last sc work.

Row 4: Ch 3 (counts as first dc now and throughout), turn, 2 dc in first ch-2 sp, *[ch 3, sc in next ch-3 sp] twice, ch 3 **, 2 dc in next ch-3 sp, dc in next dc, 2 dc in next ch-3 sp, rep from * across ending at ** on last rep, 3 dc in turning ch-sp.

Row 5: Ch 3 (counts as first dc), turn, dc in next dc, *[ch 3, sc in next ch-3 sp] 3 times, ch 3, sk 1 dc**, dc in each of next 3 dc, rep from * across ending at ** on last rep, dc in each of last 2 sts.

Row 6: Ch 6 (counts as first dc, ch 3 throughout), turn, sc in first ch-3 sp, [ch 3, sc in next ch-3 sp] 3 times, *ch 3, sk 1 dc, dc in next dc **, [ch 3, sc in next ch-3 sp] 4 times; rep from * across ending at **, ch 3, sk next dc, dc in top of turning ch.

Row 7: Ch 6 (counts as first dc, ch 3 throughout), turn, sc in first ch-3 sp, [ch 3, sc in next ch-3 sp] 4 times, *ch 3, dc in next dc, ch 3, sl st in last dc made, (picot made) [ch 3, sc in next ch-3 sp] 5 times, rep from * across, ch 3, dc in 3rd ch of turning ch-6. Fasten off.

Finishing

Weave in all ends. Block to size.

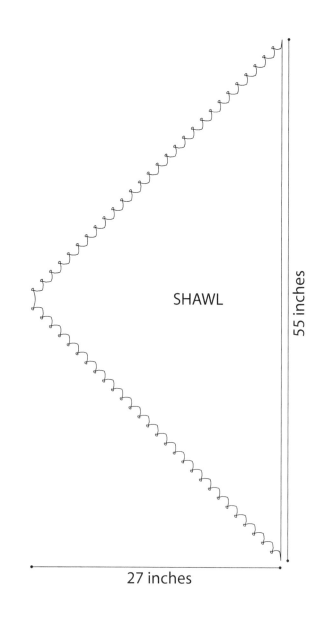

SHAWL

55 inches

27 inches

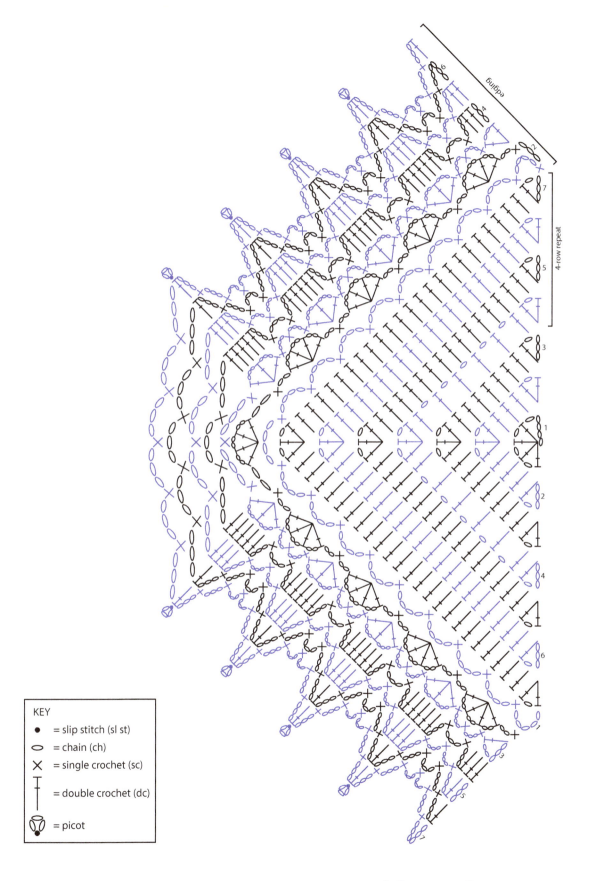

KEY
● = slip stitch (sl st)
⬭ = chain (ch)
✕ = single crochet (sc)
† = double crochet (dc)
🮲 = picot

Acknowledgments

Writing a book is tough. But I have had a team whose love and enthusiasm for me and this project has propelled me through this first "big" book I have ever done on my own.

My husband, David, has been with me on this adventure from the get-go. Thank you for understanding when the kitchen table was covered in blocking boards with shawls in various states of blocking and having to wade through the living room with even more pieces blocking there. Thank you for understanding when dinner/laundry/grocery shopping was late and how excited I got when one more box of yarn arrived. Thank you for being my rock, listening to me when I planned, dreamed, cried, and tried to figure out this whole self-publishing thing. But most of all, thank you for being you and loving me through all the crazy.

Tyler and Cassie, thank you for always "getting it." Even when I was making you bright-colored, over-sized sweaters you still loved and wore everything I made for you. Cassie, you were (and still are) the best model ever, even at age 4. Tyler, major KUDOS for allowing me 100%, no holds barred entry to your room because my stash closet is in there. And thank you for being my "helper" and now my copy editor. Now in college, you both tell everyone who will listen about your yarnie mom. I love you both to the moon and back.

Thank you to my model makers, Amy Curtin and Penny Shima Glanz. Because of both of you, not only do I have some gorgeous samples, my hands are still in great shape. Your work is incredible.

On the technical side of things, thank you to the tech editor and graphic artist behind all my stitch charts and schematics – Kj Hay. You are so amazing, wonderful and generous with your time and talent. Thanks to you I have beautifully clear and mesmerizing charts, clear and understandable patterns and you make sure that every pattern is consistent! (And the math is good!)

Also thank you to the wonderful team at Stitch Definition – Anne Podelsak for the absolutely incredible photography and Elizabeth Green for the beautiful graphic artistry of the book's layout. Both of you were on board from the moment I mentioned the idea to you and have helped me craft the image in my head into the stunning pages we see right here. My gratitude is endless!

Thank you to the absolutely stunning model, Theresa Martinez. You made every one of my designs come alive with the beauty and elegance that I wanted!

Thank you to Kathy Smith Adams, my BFF of 38 years, for helping me to realize that I can do this and encouraging me to go out on my own. Never forget – "Save the Texas Prairie Chickens!"

Thank you to my Nonna Mary Parducci for teaching me to crochet. You told me then that you had given me a skill and that I needed to do something with it. I'm not sure this is what you expected but I know that you still help me when I need it from up above. Ti amo!

Most importantly, I must thank God my Almighty Father for first showing my Nonna that He had given me this talent and inspiring her to teach me and for showing me that I could cultivate it and use it to better myself and to enrich the lives of others. "As each one has received a special gift, employ it in serving one another, as good stewards of the manifold grace of God." – 1 Peter 4:10

Resources

Yarns

Feel free to substitute yarns. If you do substitute, you must realize that you will have to verify your gauge and if you change the weight of yarn, you will almost definitely need a different amount of yarn than listed in the pattern.

Aslant uses 1300 yards Round Table Yarns Guenevere in color "My beauty will not hold."
100% superwash merino
roundtableyarns.com

Breeze uses 900 yards of Blue Moon Fiber Arts Laci in the color Midsummers Night.
100% extra fine 80's merino
Bluemoonfiberarts.com

Briar uses 1200 yards of Bare Naked Wools Chebris Lace in the color Creme.
60% fine wool / 40% yearling mohair wool
Knitspot.com

Drift uses 1100 yards of YOTH Yarns Mother in colors Spring Water, Blue Raspberry, Blueberry and Caviar.
100% domestic rambouillet wool
yothyarns.com

Ecliptic uses 750 yards of Anzula Luxury Fibers Breeze in color Persimmon.
65% silk / 35% linen
Anzula.com

Enchantment uses 1200 yards of Blue Moon Fiber Arts Yaksi Fingering in the color "True Blood" Red.
60% wool / 20% yak / 20% silk
Bluemoonfiberarts.com

Foliole uses 960 yards of The Fiber Seed Sprout in the color Sour Apple.
90% superwash merino / 10% nylon
thefiberseed.com

Incipient uses 1200 yards of The Fiber Seed Silky Seed Lace in the colors Shamrock and Dragon Fruit.
50% fine merino / 50% tussah silk
thefiberseed.com

Palisade uses 860 yards of Black Trillium Fibres Silken in the color Lemon Chiffon.
85% superwash merino / 15% mulberry silk
blacktrilliumfibres.com

Solar uses 675 yards of Black Trillium Fibres Lilt Sock Gradient Kit in the color Squash Blossom.
85% superwash merino / 15% silk
blacktrilliumfibres.com

Trellis uses 550 yards of Prism Yarns Lace Wool in the color Arroyo.
100% wool
prismyarn.com

Violaceous uses 725 yards of Happy Fuzzy Yarn Merino Silk Lace in the color Iris.
80% merino / 20% tussah silk
Happyfuzzyyarn.com

Blocking Supplies

Eucalan Delicate Wash
eucalan.com/products-1/delicate-wash

Soak Wash
Soakwash.com

Inspinknity, LLC, Blocking Wires
inspinknity.com

Anti Rust T-Pins
amzn.to/2deIxQP
(affiliate link)

About the Author

Crochet Hooks

Addi® Comfort Grip Hooks
www.skacelknitting.com/
Addi-Comfort-Grip-Hook-
Color-Coded-Handle

Notions

Magnetic Chart Keeper
knitpicks.com/accessories/
Knitting_Chart_Keep-
er__D80314.html

Highlighter Tape
amzn.to/2d2Q6NV
(affiliate link)

Photo by Craftsy

Karen Whooley teaches classes and develops patterns for adventurous crocheters who want simplicity and elegance. With the reputation of having clean, simple patterns that are easy to read she is the author of numerous books and is a sought after instructor worldwide. Karen is a professional member of The Crochet Guild of America (CGOA) and a Creative Business Services member of The National NeedleArts Association (TNNA). She and her husband, David, live in Everett, Washington, and enjoy the beautiful Pacific Northwest. Her website is www.KarenWhooley.com.

CPSIA information can be obtained
at www.ICGtesting.com
Printed in the USA
BVHW02s1532220318
511186BV00014B/280/P